# The World of
# Gymnastics

# The World of
# Gymnastics

### Edited by
## Peter Tatlow

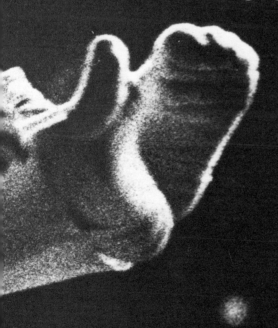

## Atheneum Publishers·New York

### Editor's Acknowledgements

Many people in the gymnastics field have been of invaluable assistance to me in the preparation of this book but in particular I should like to thank Nik Stuart, Meg Warren and Tony Murdock for their advice during the initial stages of the planning of the book. It has been my great pleasure to work with all the contributors, all of whom are leading personalities on the gymnastics scene, and I feel that their joining together has given the reader a truly international survey of gymnastics. The publishers would like to acknowledge the help given by Christopher Pick in the editing of the movements section and Minot Simons II who acted in an advisory capacity over American terminology and practices.

Nadia Comaneci (Rumania)

*Page 1:* Shigeru Kasamatsu of Japan
*Page 2-3:* Volker Rohrwick of West Germany

First American edition published 1978 by Atheneum Publishers, New York

Library of Congress Cataloging in Publication Data

Main entry under title:

The World of gymnastics.

    Includes index.
    1. Gymnastics—Addresses, essays, lectures.
I. Tatlow, Peter.
GV461.W67    1978    796.4′1    78-5389
ISBN 0-689-10899-0

Designed and produced by Walter Parrish International Limited

Printed and bound in Great Britain by Purnell & Sons Ltd

# Contents

Avril Lennox (Great Britain)

Peter Kormann (United States)

# Editor's Introduction

Often I am asked what gymnastics means to me and I suppose it must be that the sport has the perfect combination of my own chief enthusiasms—theatre and music, live entertainment, and games of all sorts. I tread on dangerous ground here, because the world gymnastics fraternity, for whom I have the most profound admiration, does not care much for the comparison with the theatre, still less with the circus and its tricks.

On the circus, I agree. The trend in artistic gymnastics towards tricks for their own sake is to be deprecated, and tricks are well looked after by Sports Acrobatics. But the association with the best of theatre strikes me as a fair comparison, because gymnastics has aestheticism, elegance, balletic beauty and dynamism, virtuosity, originality, and strength of mind and body.

Sitting in the press box at stadia and gymnasia I derive constant satisfaction from the graceful musical and theatrical movements I see before me. The fact that it is competitive is an extra bonus.

What could be more elegant than balances, pirouettes, rolls, cartwheels, and somersaults correctly performed? When they are done by the likes of Ludmilla Tourischeva, Elvira Saadi, Nelli Kim, Olga Korbut, Vera Caslavska or Nadia Comaneci, among the women, or with the power of such men as Nikolai Andrianov, Mitsuo Tsukahara or Zoltan Magyar, to mention but a few, you have examples of truly sublime body movements.

After the exciting progress in technique and originality of the last twenty years, a few worries arise for the future. Once upon a time only one athlete had run the four-minute mile: now many do. Once upon a time only one gymnast had performed the Yamashita vault: now everyone can, but few do because it is downgraded to a 9.40 tariff. And rapidly the twisting Tsukahara vault is going the same way, together with triple back saltos. What is the limit of the human frame? Are we moving from aestheticism and strength towards mere virtuosity?

Olga Korbut caught the imagination of the world at the Munich Olympics in 1972 because, following on the Vera Caslavska era, the television cameras focused for the first time on gymnastics. Since Korbut retired the excited fans still pour into stadia throughout the world, but often the magic atmosphere that she, and now Comaneci, command is missing. Meanwhile the quality of men's gymnastics is increasing all the while, and the men now need a star of the stature of the balletic John Curry from the ice-skating world.

However, such musings aside, if you are one of the millions who thrill to the highlights of world gymnastics competition on television or in the stadium, or are eagerly taking up the sport for yourself in school or club gymnasium, I hope you will find in the words, photographs and movement drawings that follow an informative and absorbing picture of the great sport itself and its practice all over the world.

# The Sport of Gymnastics

## The Origins of Gymnastics

Gymnastics consists of an infinite variety of movements on various pieces of apparatus and on the floor and calls for ingenuity, skill and an ability to combine both harmoniously.

Observation of apes, monkeys and the lower animal forms indicates that climbing, hanging, balancing and tumbling—all basic gymnastic activities—are engaged in by young animals and undoubtedly prehistoric and early man participated in these activities for enjoyment as well as for the all-important purposes of hunting for food and escaping his enemies.

Ancient records found in China, Persia and Egypt describe—sometimes in words and sometimes in pictures—how the skills that form the very basics of gymnastics were practised long ago in those countries. Mostly this was for the purpose of providing well-conditioned, physically tough soldiers for the army.

*Above:* An illustration of a medieval tumbler. It would give today's judge much food for thought and opportunity for technical deduction.

In Ancient Greece physical training played an important part in the lives of all young males. The Greeks believed that they should be proficient in all phases of life and that the physical played an important part in developing the whole person. The word 'Gymnastics' is derived from the Greek *Gymnos,* meaning nude, reflecting the practice of Greeks to participate unclothed, and so gymnastics literally means 'the naked art'. Because of their love of physical activities, the Greeks developed the Olympic Games, which remained in existence for 1100 years. They took place in Olympia, where the temple of Zeus cast its shadow across the open-air stadium, and the young men wrestled and raced for the coveted wreaths from the olive tree that Hercules was supposed to have planted. In the Olympiad of 776 BC gymnastics provided the build-up for the disciplined physique and mobile body which was so essential in the sporting arena and was a requirement of full Greek citizenship. In those days only athletes born and bred in Greece could take part. In the games, apparatus in the form of spears, slings and arrows were used and gymnastics embraced many events such as boxing, throwing, wrestling, jumping and weight lifting.

The Romans adopted from the Greeks the phases of gymnastics they believed of military value. They used the wooden horse,

This photograph of a Danish gymnast at the 1908 Olympics in Helsinki serves to illustrate changes in dress, equipment and type of performance since the early days of international gymnastics.

Vaulting over a real horse in a seventeenth-century German handbill advertising the activities of an acrobatic troupe.

which they mounted and dismounted; this has come to be the side horse and long horse of modern gymnastics.

Physical culture declined with the fall of the Greek and Roman empires and throughout the Middle Ages the only groups following courses of physical exercise were knights and warriors, who enjoyed jousting and other field sports, and tumblers in the theatre.

Modern competitive gymnastics as we know it today started in the late 18th century in central Europe. The revival of the discipline of physical exercise came about because educationists saw the sport as an integral part of the school curriculum. The leaders of the theory were, in Germany, Johann Basedow (1723-90), Johann Guts Muths (1759-1818) and Gerhard Vieth (1763-1836) and, in Switzerland, Johann Pestalozzi (1746-1827).

That early lead was soon to be radically developed by Friedrich Jahn, a German, and Pehr Ling, a Swede. They became the parents of artistic gymnastics through two completely different systems.

Friedrich Ludwig Jahn (1778-1852) was born in Lanz near Wittenberg and served in the Prussian army. In 1811 he set up a gymnastics school near Berlin. He is known as the *Turnvater* (father of gymnastics) because he started a system of *Turnen* (gymnastics) from which the *Turnverein* (Gymnastics Societies) arose and eventually spread to England and the United States. In the United States, the original impetus came in the 1880s with the advent of immigrants from Europe. Gymnastics societies were founded by them and played a large part in the athletic programmes in schools and colleges. Jahn is credited with inventing the horizontal bar, parallel bars, pommelled horse, balance beam, ladders and vaulting equipment. He did not promote his brand of gymnastics in schools but developed it rather as a programme for adults and adolescents outside the schools.

Pehr Henrik Ling (1776-1839) introduced his system of gymnastics in Sweden. He saw it as physical education for the masses, starting in the schools. To him it was a body builder for the weak as well as the strong and he combined this aspect with a deep understanding of the effect movement had on the human body. His philosophy was safety first and the emphasis of his system was group instruction at a word of command. Ling objected strongly to Jahn's method of difficult and sometimes violent movements which could lead to injury.

The two systems—Ling's desire for the perfect rhythm of movement mainly on the floor which was introduced in England in 1879 and the United States in 1889, and Jahn's muscular development for moving the body around fixed apparatus—were diametrically opposed to each other. In the early 1920s the world governing body, the International Federation of Gymnastics, founded in 1881, went a long way towards bringing the two systems together, but even today there is still a clash of aims between purely physical education and artistic gymnastics.

The countries that have shown the strongest performance in competitive gymnastics in recent years are Japan, the Soviet Union, the United States, Great Britain, East and West Germany, Switzerland, Czechoslovakia, and Rumania. All these countries have good, sound training programmes which nurture talent and develop gymnasts of international calibre from school level upwards.

*Opposite:* Olga Korbut in one of the extraordinary poses for which she is famous.

*Page 10:* Sakiko Nozawa of Japan performing a body wave on the beam at the 1977 'Champions All' in London.

# Olga and Nadia:
# the Gymnastics Explosion

The phenomenal current boom in the sport of gymnastics can be put down to two names: Olga and Nadia. Between them, these two elfin girls, Olga Korbut and Nadia Comaneci, who are immediately identifiable both inside the sport and out by their forenames alone, have sparked off the ambitions of millions of teenage and pre-teenage girls throughout the world.

They come from different countries, and have rarely competed against each other, and yet without them gymnastics might still be a struggling minority sport instead of a huge growth activity, with gymnastics clubs inundated with membership applications.

But how, in the half-dozen years since the 1972 Munich Olympics, has this come about? The story probably begins at the Sporthalle in Munich on Monday 28 August, when a tiny Soviet girl named Olga Korbut was shedding some of the most famous teardrops in sporting history.

Olga, just 4 feet 11 inches tall and weighing around 84 pounds, was the smallest member of the mighty Soviet gymnastics team, for so long supreme in women's gymnastics. She was the one who marched in at the end of the line, with a huge team shoulder bag almost hiding her from view. Like all the Russians in Munich, she was an excellent gymnast, and she introduced a new element of daring to the sport with her backward somersault on the four-inch-wide beam.

In the Olympic All Around competition, Olga performed well. But on the uneven parallel (asymmetric) bars she made two mistakes which ruined her performance. Her mark—which on earlier apparatus had been no lower than 9.4 out of 10—plummeted to 7.5.

The heartbroken Olga slumped onto a chair, covered her face with her hands, and began sobbing bitterly. At that moment, hundreds of millions of television viewers all over

*Page 11:* Ron Gallimore, America's top floor exercise worker, on the side horse, performing a front round.

*Opposite:* Hisato Igarashi, fast rising star of Japanese gymnastics, in the half lever at the *Chunichi* Cup in Tokyo. He is built in the same mould as Tsukahara and Kenmotsu and is an obvious challenger for future Olympic and World titles.

The sport of gymnastics will always be the sport which Olga Korbut made unforgettable. This photograph shows one of her unique movements outside the normal field of competitive gymnastics.

the world were watching the Olympic gymnastics, and the close-up pictures of the crestfallen Russian, her gold medal hopes in tatters, melted the hearts of young and old alike.

But the story had a happy ending. Olga went on to win her Olympic gold medals in the team event, the individual floor exercise and the balance beam, together with a silver medal for the uneven parallel (asymmetric) bars. The Munich Olympics had shown the tiny Olga to be not only a superb gymnast, but a very human one too.

From this interest in Olga there stemmed a curiosity about her background, and although it was not untypical of Soviet athletes, it seemed a new world to most people. The unseen training, dedication—and pain which accompany such brilliance came to the surface, and sparked off among many youngsters the desire to emulate Olga. They even tied their hair in the Olga Korbut way.

For several years following the Munich Olympics, Olga Korbut remained the star name in gymnastics, attracting huge crowds wherever she appeared.

It was widely felt that she would be the star

personality gymnast of the 1976 Montreal Olympics too, until, in 1975, a new star burst upon the scene. She came from Rumania, a country where, some years earlier, the decline of standards in the sport had caused the government to launch a big campaign to discover and develop gymnastics talent.

The first 'star' to emerge from this campaign, Nadia Comaneci, won the British Amateur Gymnastics Association's 'Champions All' tournament at Wembley, London, in April 1975, when she was just 13 years old. It was her first contest in the West.

Nadia, at a shade under 5 feet in height and weighing around 84 pounds, was just about the same build as Olga at Munich.

She did not have the same extrovert nature as Olga, but she was a superb gymnast, and everyone wanted a confrontation between her and Olga. It came at the Montreal Olympics, and Olga, reluctantly, had to hand over the crown as chief crowd-pleaser to the little Rumanian. Nadia won three golds, a silver and a bronze, became overall Olympic champion, and was the only girl to qualify for the finals of all four individual pieces of apparatus. She was also the first gymnast at the Olympics to score 10 out of 10 and she achieved it seven times. A new queen reigned.

Since those momentous days, Olga Korbut has retired from gymnastics and Rumania has cast a shadow over the success of Nadia Comaneci by walking out as a team from the European Championships in Prague in 1977. But they have a place in history, and the rapid growth of gymnastics since 1972 means the sport owes more to Olga and Nadia than it could ever repay.

Nadia Comaneci preparing for her famous dismount, the shoot half turn back somersault, which she brought to perfection at Montreal in 1976.

# Sponsorship for an Amateur Sport

Many sports today rely heavily on sponsorship from large companies wishing to promote their products. Gymnastics is no exception.

Sponsorship relates primarily to putting on major tournaments and competitions. Sponsors include newspapers and broadcasting companies, beverage producers and organizations, and a soap manufacturer. In the Soviet Union, the *Moscow News* newspaper sponsors a tournament in April which has become important for younger gymnasts. In Japan, the newspaper *Chunichi* sponsors a major international tournament, held in November, which provides the Japanese Gymnastics Federation with its major source of revenue; in addition, Japan's largest broadcasting company, the Nippon Broadcasting Corporation, sponsors a tournament, usually held in mid-June, which, like the *Moscow News* event, is mainly directed towards younger gymnasts. In Great Britain, the *Daily Mirror* sponsors a major competition for the very top athletes, the 'Champions All' tournament; the *Daily Mirror* also sends gymnasts to the Soviet Union every year for training. It is the policy of the British Amateur Gymnastics Association never to take on more than one sponsor from a particular category. The *Daily Mirror,* for instance, is the only daily newspaper; the *Sunday Times,* the only Sunday newspaper and Lilia-White, the only feminine hygiene product company, sponsoring gymnastic events. The newest sponsors in Great Britain are Outline (Low Fat Spread) and Coca Cola. Coca Cola has inaugurated a major tournament in December. In Canada, Coca Cola and the Milk Marketing Board sponsor a major international tournament in November.

In the United States, the Dial Soap Company has undertaken to support the United States Gymnastics Federation in a number of events annually. The agreement is for one year at a time, but three years are inferred, so that the Federation can build a programme for the 1980 Olympics. If all goes well, Dial will put more than a million dollars into American gymnastics during the period 1977-80. This sum will compensate, for example, for the expense of sending gymnasts to events overseas. These missions are a total loss, financially, as the sending country receives no income. Experience is gained, of course, but only the host country derives income from television rights and the sale of tickets. This heavy participation in American gymnastics by a major manufacturer will help to offset the advantage of government support enjoyed by communist countries.

For the past twenty or thirty years, however, long before the entry of Dial into the sponsorship picture, the equipment manufacturers have been the major supporters of American gymnastics. Unlike those organizations that sponsor one particular event every year, or Dial that provides an annual financial grant, the contributions of the equipment companies vary from year to year. The Nissen Company, for example, underwrote foreign tours before the days of Olga Korbut when such tours were not always profitable. Nissen underwrote the national championships of the American Athletics Union three years in a row and now underwrites the annual Independent Club Championships. They state flatly that they will provide equipment for any meet that needs it. This commitment may require them to provide equipment for more than fifty competitions in a year.

The American Athletic Equipment Division of A.M.F. prefers to restrict its sponsorship to national events such as the American Cup or major events like the Rumania versus the United States meet.

The involvement of Nissen and A.M.F. in American gymnastics runs deep. Private clubs, however, do not as a rule have recourse to sponsors for the financial costs of a local meet. They must depend upon the sale of tickets, advertising in meet programmes and promotional activities of their own design.

The rewards to a sponsor are primarily those of advertising and public relations. In gymnastics, the growth in the number of sponsors must mean that the derived exposure is considered worth the expense. Hopefully, therefore, sponsorship will continue to grow and to reach down to lower levels of gymnastics competition.

## Organizing a Worldwide Sport: the International Federation of Gymnastics

The International Federation of Gymnastics, known universally as the F.I.G. (the initials of its French name), founded in Liège by the Belgian Nicolas Cupérus in 1881 and at that time uniting the gymnastics federations of Belgium, France and Holland, today comprises no fewer than seventy-four national associations from the five continents. The first years were beset with problems and it was only at the turn of the 20th century, when eighteen European federations joined and the New World was represented for the first time by Canada, that the Federation became more than just a good idea.

There were five chief aims which the Federation proclaimed at that time: (1) to exchange official documents and publications; (2) to set up a procedure for invitations among members; (3) not to recognize federations pursuing political or religious aims; (4) to ban professionals from competitions; (5) to organize international competitions. The last point, the establishing of comprehensive rules and principles for the execution of international tournaments, was the most important. The foundation for this was laid in the house of Nicolas Cupérus, the President of the Federation, in the presence of the Frenchman Cazalet and the Dutchman Müller. The first international gymnastics tournament organized by the F.I.G. took place in Antwerp in 1903 and this represented an important milestone. Besides the Benelux countries, France also took part, with Italy and Hungary showing a definite interest.

In those days, all-round ability was the fundamental law of gymnastics, the events required not being limited to apparatus work but also embracing three light-athletic events such as sprint, high jump, long jump, pole

Some of the all-round activities, including pole-vaulting and rope-climbing, that were part of gymnastics before the development of pure artistic gymnastics, in an early German print.

*Opposite:* Yuri Titov, then only 21, made an unforgettable impression on world gymnastics in Melbourne in 1956. Now, as President of the International Federation of Gymnastics, he is making an impression on gymnasts all over the world.

vault, shot put, weight lifting or rope climbing—to mention just a few. Certain exercises had to be done as a group display. Such tournaments took place every two years until the start of World War I. Some countries participated in the Olympic Games and here, at any rate, pure artistic gymnastics played a larger part in the competitions.

The pre-war tournaments resumed in 1922 in Ljubljana but this era finally came to an end with the tournament in Paris in 1930, when it was decided to have a go at full-scale world competitions.

Impetus was given to this decision by the positive development of pure artistic gymnastics and by the numerical increase of the membership of the F.I.G. following the entry of the U.S.A. and other overseas and European countries, among them Finland, Switzerland and Denmark. The Germans kept out for another year but, remembering they had to organize the gymnastics competitions of the Olympic Games in 1936, they joined in 1934.

The first World Championships took place in Budapest in 1934. The men had the 15-event competition and there were twelve countries taking part. Women from five countries also took part, but only in the group exhibition. The success of these World Championships led to the second in Prague in 1938 which, however, were beset with political troubles in the shadow of impending World War II. Yet the F.I.G. managed to stage this meet with eight countries (eight men's teams turned out, all from Europe). Once again it included the 15-event competition, and so did the third World Championships in Basle, the first international meet after the war, although this time only six countries took part. This was the last time the 15-event programme was included. At the congress in Basle the decision was taken to strike from the programme all events that were not pure artistic gymnastics. Women also participated for the first time in both the group and individual events. The post-war years gave rise to a more and more intensive development in technique and performance which helped to swell the F.I.G.'s membership rolls. (By this time there were twenty-nine federations from four continents.)

At the 14th Olympiad in London in 1948 there was much innovation and the gymnasts from the U.S.A. were in with a good chance for the first time.

In the Helsinki games in 1952 the men and women of the Soviet Union, making their first appearances, made it clear that the easy-going attitude of the past was over and an era of strongly competitive gymnastics was on its way. Even the Japanese impressed the gymnastics world with their splendid performance. They showed much originality combined with good technique, so that it was already a good guess that they would soon lead the world in men's gymnastics.

Without doubt, the Soviet Union and Japan gave a new dimension both to gymnastics and to the F.I.G. and created a transition to a new, high level of development. This prompted the F.I.G. to appoint a technical president to be responsible for new projects, for instance the standardization and improvement of apparatus and judging rules.

Since 1948 the F.I.G. has directed its attention towards regulating judging into a system and ensuring reliable scoring. To this end, there appeared in 1949 the first Code of Points, and a more elaborate Code was produced for the World Championships in 1954, also to be implemented in the Olympic programme. The Code included the addition of A, B and C parts for men, intended as categories of progressive difficulty (see page 28). The essential standards of certain apparatus were prescribed and rules were set out for the scheduling of competitions.

Apart from the emergence of the Soviet Union and Japan as gymnastic giants, the 1950s also saw the spread of gymnastics all over the world. Sixteen congresses of the International Federation had taken place by 1930 and in the next thirty years the total reached twenty-three, with a further ten added by 1970. Every year there is an F.I.G. congress with new problems to discuss and decisions to be made and every year there is a large-scale F.I.G. event—Olympic Games, World Championships, European Championships—or other regional competitions under the technical supervision of the F.I.G., like the Pan-American or the Mediterranean Games. With the increasing popularity of gymnastics throughout the world, today's F.I.G. officials, who are unpaid, certainly have to be devoted to the sport.

# Competitive Gymnastics

## The Anatomy of International Competitions

Many of the seventy-four nations which belong to the F.I.G. conduct regional competitions on an annual or semi-annual basis. The European Championships, for example, will soon be held yearly, with the event every other year being for junior gymnasts only. The Pan-American Games include competitions in a multitude of sports, among them gymnastics, and these games are under the direct supervision of the Olympic Committees of the participating nations. In the past the World Championships were held every four years, spaced between the Olympic Games which were also held every four years. This provided the truly world-class gymnast with a major event every other year. Beginning in 1979, however, the World Championships will be conducted every two years and the event held the year directly before the Olympic Games (i.e. the next will be in 1979) will determine the top twelve teams for the following Olympics. Nations wishing to host such official championships submit their bids to the F.I.G. The F.I.G. evaluates the bids and makes recommendations to the membership. The successful country is appointed to host the event at the annual F.I.G. congress. Judges are chosen from nations who belong to the F.I.G. and must be qualified according to certification tests administered by the F.I.G.'s men's and women's technical committees.

At the Olympics and the World Championships three different competitions are staged, the Team Competition, the Individual All Around Finals and the Individual Event Finals.

### Competition 1: Team Competition

There are six gymnasts to a team and men and women have their own separate competitions. The men work six apparatus (floor, pommelled horse, still rings, long horse, parallel bars and horizontal bar) and the women four (broad horse, uneven parallel (asymmetric) bars, balance beam and floor).

At every apparatus the five top scores count towards the team total or, to put it another way, the lowest score is crossed off.

In the Team Competition gymnasts first do compulsory exercises on each apparatus. These are routines set by the F.I.G. for four-year periods and they must be performed in the stipulated sequence; they always include similar activities but in varying combinations. The compulsories are followed by voluntary exercises (optionals). These are the routines the gymnasts work out for themselves.

The total score possible in a team event is 600 points for men and 400 for women. This is

Ludmilla Tourischeva, dowager queen of gymnastics, with her four golds at the World Cup in London in 1975.

worked out from the following formula. A gymnast can score ten points at every apparatus so five (of the six) gymnasts could score fifty points for the team. There are six pieces of apparatus, and compulsory and voluntary exercises for each. 10 points × 5 gymnasts × 6 apparatus × 2 = 600 points.

*Key to abbreviations:* V—Vault; UPB—Uneven Parallel (asymmetric) Bars; B—Beam; FX—Floor Exercises; PH—Pommelled Horse; R—Rings; PB—Parallel Bar; HB—Horizontal Bar; C—Compulsory Exercises; O—Optional or Voluntary Exercises.

*Table A:* two top women's and men's results in the Team Competition in the 1976 Montreal Olympics.

## Table A

### Women

| TEAM-Name | Place | V | UPB | B | FX | C&O Total | Final Total |
|---|---|---|---|---|---|---|---|
| SOVIET UNION (URS) | C | 48.70 | 48.85 | 47.95 | 48.70 | 194.20 | |
| | O | 49.00 | 49.00 | 48.95 | 49.20 | 196.15 | 390.35 |
| Kim, Nelli | 2 | 9.80 | 9.80 | 9.40 | 9.80 | 38.80 | |
| | | 9.90 | 9.85 | 9.80 | 9.90 | 39.45 | 78.25 |
| Tourischeva, Ludmilla | 2 | 9.80 | 9.75 | 9.40 | 9.90 | 38.85 | |
| | | 9.80 | 9.80 | 9.85 | 9.95 | 39.40 | 78.25 |
| Korbut, Olga | 5 | 9.75 | 9.90 | 9.80 | 9.35 | 38.80 | |
| | | 9.70 | 9.90 | 9.85 | 9.70 | 39.15 | 77.95 |
| Saadi, Elvira | 7 | 9.70 | 9.70 | 9.55 | 9.70 | 38.65 | |
| | | 9.70 | 9.70 | 9.70 | 9.70 | 38.80 | 77.45 |
| Filatova, Maria | 9 | 9.65 | 9.50 | 9.30 | 9.50 | 37.95 | |
| | | 9.90 | 9.60 | 9.75 | 9.85 | 39.10 | 77.05 |
| Grozdova, Svetlana | 9 | 9.50 | 9.70 | 9.80 | 9.80 | 38.80 | |
| | | 9.50 | 9.75 | 9.20 | 9.80 | 38.25 | 77.05 |
| ROMANIA (ROM) | C | 47.95 | 49.15 | 48.05 | 47.55 | 192.70 | |
| | O | 48.05 | 49.35 | 48.80 | 48.25 | 194.45 | 387.15 |
| Comaneci, Nadia | 1 | 9.70 | 10.00 | 9.90 | 9.75 | 39.35 | |
| | | 9.85 | 10.00 | 10.00 | 9.85 | 39.70 | 79.05 |
| Ungureanu, Teodora | 4 | 9.65 | 9.90 | 9.75 | 9.55 | 38.85 | |
| | | 9.70 | 9.90 | 9.85 | 9.75 | 39.20 | 78.05 |
| Constantin, Mariana | 14 | 9.55 | 9.85 | 9.45 | 9.35 | 38.15 | |
| | | 9.65 | 9.85 | 9.60 | 9.50 | 38.60 | 76.75 |
| Grigoras, Anca | 15 | 9.45 | 9.65 | 9.60 | 9.45 | 38.15 | |
| | | 9.50 | 9.75 | 9.75 | 9.55 | 38.55 | 76.70 |
| Trusca, Gabriela | 18 | 9.65 | 9.75 | 9.30 | 9.30 | 38.00 | |
| | | 9.25 | 9.85 | 9.60 | 9.40 | 38.10 | 76.10 |
| Gabor, Georgeta | 21 | 9.30 | 9.50 | 9.35 | 9.45 | 37.60 | |
| | | 9.35 | 9.60 | 9.55 | 9.60 | 38.10 | 75.70 |

### Men

| TEAM-Name | Place | FX | PH | R | V | PB | HB | C&O Total | Final Total |
|---|---|---|---|---|---|---|---|---|---|
| JAPAN (JPN) | C | 47.20 | 47.70 | 47.20 | 47.80 | 48.15 | 48.25 | 286.30 | |
| | O | 47.95 | 48.70 | 48.65 | 47.85 | 48.30 | 49.10 | 290.55 | 576.85 |
| Kato, Sawao | 2 | 9.50 | 9.60 | 9.45 | 9.55 | 9.75 | 9.65 | 57.50 | |
| | | 9.70 | 9.80 | 9.80 | 9.55 | 9.80 | 9.75 | 58.40 | 115.90 |
| Tsukahara, Mitsuo | 3 | 9.50 | 9.50 | 9.45 | 9.50 | 9.70 | 9.75 | 57.40 | |
| | | 9.55 | 9.70 | 9.75 | 9.80 | 9.65 | 9.90 | 58.35 | 115.75 |
| Kajiyama, Hiroshi | 5 | 9.45 | 9.50 | 9.40 | 9.65 | 9.70 | 9.50 | 57.20 | |
| | | 9.50 | 9.75 | 9.70 | 9.70 | 9.65 | 9.75 | 58.05 | 115.25 |
| Kenmotsu, Eizo | 6 | 9.45 | 9.70 | 9.55 | 9.65 | 9.00 | 9.65 | 57.00 | |
| | | 9.65 | 9.85 | 9.70 | 9.35 | 9.75 | 9.85 | 58.15 | 115.15 |
| Igarashi, Hisato | 15 | 9.00 | 9.40 | 9.25 | 9.45 | 9.55 | 9.60 | 56.25 | |
| | | 9.45 | 9.60 | 9.50 | 9.45 | 9.45 | 9.85 | 57.30 | 113.55 |
| Fujimoto, Shun | 89 | 9.30 | 9.10 | 9.35 | 9.00 | 0.00 | 0.00 | 28.75 | |
| | | 9.55 | 9.50 | 9.70 | 0.00 | 0.00 | 0.00 | 55.80 | 84.55 |
| SOVIET UNION (URS) | C | 47.80 | 48.00 | 48.00 | 47.60 | 47.70 | 47.70 | 286.80 | |
| | O | 48.80 | 47.90 | 49.35 | 47.60 | 47.60 | 48.40 | 289.65 | 576.45 |
| Andrianov, Nikolai | 1 | 9.45 | 9.70 | 9.80 | 9.65 | 9.80 | 9.70 | 58.10 | |
| | | 9.85 | 9.75 | 9.90 | 9.70 | 9.70 | 9.50 | 58.40 | 116.50 |
| Markelov, Vladimir | 4 | 9.70 | 9.60 | 9.70 | 9.60 | 9.65 | 9.60 | 57.85 | |
| | | 9.75 | 9.40 | 9.90 | 9.20 | 9.60 | 9.70 | 57.55 | 115.40 |
| Ditiatin, Alexandr | 6 | 9.60 | 9.65 | 9.60 | 9.40 | 9.50 | 9.45 | 57.20 | |
| | | 9.70 | 9.65 | 9.90 | 9.65 | 9.40 | 9.65 | 57.95 | 115.15 |
| Kryssin, Gennadi | 8 | 9.50 | 9.45 | 9.30 | 9.50 | 9.45 | 9.50 | 56.70 | |
| | | 9.70 | 9.55 | 9.60 | 9.50 | 9.40 | 9.80 | 57.55 | 114.25 |
| Marchenko, Vladimir | 11 | 9.55 | 9.60 | 9.50 | 9.45 | 8.55 | 9.60 | 56.10 | |
| | | 9.80 | 9.45 | 9.85 | 9.55 | 9.50 | 9.60 | 57.75 | 113.85 |
| Tikhonov, Vladimir | 23 | 9.40 | 9.40 | 9.40 | 9.40 | 9.30 | 9.30 | 56.20 | |
| | | 9.55 | 9.50 | 9.80 | 8.65 | 8.80 | 9.65 | 55.95 | 112.15 |

The formula for women is similar. 10 points × 5 gymnasts × 4 apparatus × 2 = 400 points. This can be studied in Table A opposite.

As we can see from the Soviet Union women's results, the total team scores for both compulsory and voluntary exercises at each apparatus are given at the top of each column. These are the totals that are added together to make the team total of 390.35. It is the scores of the top five gymnasts at every apparatus that become the team total.

As a further illustration of this point let us take the compulsory women's score in the vault—48.70. If we look down the same column at the first of the two scores for each gymnast we find that Svetlana Grozdova had the lowest at 9.50, so her score was crossed off for the purpose of the team total. If we now add up Kim (9.80), Tourischeva (9.80), Korbut (9.75), Saadi (9.70), and Filatova (9.65) we get 48.70. Adding across from left to right we get 194.20 for the compulsories and 196.15 for the optionals for the Russian women's

The back somersault on the beam, first performed by Olga Korbut at the Munich Olympics in 1972. Perfectionists still fault the technique, but only in retrospect. She was an innovator, and innovators have a special licence.

winning team score of 390.35. For that they all won gold team medals only. No individual medals are won in Competition 1.

**Competition 2: Individual All Around Finals**
This consists of voluntary exercises at every apparatus. Compulsories are worked only in the Team Competition.

The competition is restricted to thirty-six gymnasts from all countries. In the Montreal Olympics the F.I.G. ruled that only three gymnasts from each country could go on to Competition 2. If that had not been the ruling, then the top six countries would have taken most of the places. As it was, Belgium, Holland, Great Britain and Italy all had a representative in Competition 2, which decides who is the Olympic Individual Champion.

The marking system for Competition 2 is as follows. Men have a possible 60 points (10 points × 6 apparatus) and women 40 points. To whatever they score in Competition 2 is added half of their individual score in Competition 1.

Half the team individual total added to the Individual All Around Finals score gives a maximum of 120 points for men and 80 points for women.

We can see from the women's results in Table B below that Nadia Comaneci scored 9.85 for her vault, 10 for her uneven parallel (asymmetric) bars, 10 for her beam and 9.90 for floor exercises, a total of 39.75. In the next column is the figure 39.525. How is this figure arrived at? If we look back to Competition 1 under Rumania we find Comaneci scored 79.05. Half of this added to 39.75 gives 79.275, the score that made Nadia Comaneci the Olympic Champion with Nelli Kim second and Ludmilla Tourischeva third.

## Competition 3: Individual Event Finals

Like the preceding competition, this consists of voluntary exercises only. It decides who is the champion at every individual piece of apparatus. The Code of Points says 'the six best gymnasts from Competition 1 will perform their optional exercises in each event.'

*Top:Table B:* results of the women's and men's Individual All Around Finals at the 1976 Montreal Olympics. *Bottom: Table C:* results of the women's and men's Individual Event Finals.

### Table B

#### Women

| | | | V | UPB | B | FX | AA Total | Prelim Total | FINAL TOTAL |
|---|---|---|---|---|---|---|---|---|---|
| 1. | Comaneci, Nadia | ROM | 9.85 | 10.00 | 10.00 | 9.90 | 39.75 | 39.525 | 79.275 |
| 2. | Kim, Nelli | URS | 10.00 | 9.90 | 9.70 | 9.95 | 39.55 | 39.125 | 78.675 |
| 3. | Tourischeva, Ludmilla | URS | 9.95 | 9.80 | 9.85 | 9.90 | 39.50 | 39.125 | 78.625 |
| 4. | Ungureanu, Teodora | ROM | 9.75 | 9.90 | 9.90 | 9.80 | 39.35 | 39.025 | 78.375 |
| 5. | Korbut, Olga | URS | 9.80 | 9.90 | 9.50 | 9.85 | 39.05 | 38.975 | 78.025 |
| 6. | Escher, Gitta | GDR | 9.90 | 9.85 | 9.55 | 9.65 | 38.95 | 38.800 | 77.750 |
| 7. | Egervari, Marta | HUN | 9.90 | 9.90 | 9.35 | 9.65 | 38.80 | 38.525 | 77.325 |
| 8. | Kische, Marion | GDR | 9.75 | 9.80 | 9.10 | 9.70 | 38.35 | 38.600 | 76.950 |
| 9. | Gerschau, Kerstin | GDR | 9.65 | 9.75 | 9.65 | 9.25 | 38.30 | 38.500 | 76.800 |
| 10. | Pohludkova, Anna | TCH | 9.50 | 9.75 | 9.50 | 9.80 | 38.55 | 38.225 | 76.775 |
| 11. | Constantin, Mariana | ROM | 9.80 | 9.80 | 9.00 | 9.65 | 38.25 | 38.375 | 76.625 |
| 12. | Bieger, Andrea | GER | 9.70 | 9.70 | 9.30 | 9.60 | 38.30 | 37.975 | 76.275 |
| 13. | Medveczky, Kriszta | HUN | 9.70 | 9.30 | 9.30 | 9.60 | 37.90 | 38.075 | 75.975 |
| 14. | Chace, Kimberly | USA | 9.50 | 9.70 | 9.45 | 9.50 | 38.15 | 37.725 | 75.875 |
| 15. | Knopova, Jana | TCH | 9.40 | 9.60 | 9.60 | 9.65 | 38.25 | 37.550 | 75.800 |
| 16. | Holkovicova, Ingrid | TCH | 9.75 | 9.70 | 8.90 | 9.60 | 37.95 | 37.800 | 75.750 |
| 17. | Toth, Margit | HUN | 9.50 | 9.75 | 8.75 | 9.55 | 37.55 | 38.025 | 75.575 |
| 17. | Willcox, Debra | USA | 9.60 | 9.45 | 9.25 | 9.50 | 37.80 | 37.525 | 75.325 |
| 18. | Wolfsberger, Leslie | USA | 9.40 | 9.60 | 9.45 | 9.55 | 38.00 | 37.325 | 75.325 |
| 20. | Hironaka, Miyuki | JPN | 9.55 | 9.50 | 9.30 | 9.45 | 37.80 | 37.500 | 75.300 |
| 21. | Chatarova, Nadia | BUL | 9.80 | 9.75 | 9.10 | 9.40 | 38.20 | 36.950 | 75.150 |
| 22. | Smulders, Ans | HOL | 9.45 | 9.70 | 9.20 | 9.45 | 37.80 | 37.300 | 75.100 |
| 23. | Bucci, Stefania | ITA | 9.45 | 9.45 | 9.50 | 9.60 | 37.85 | 37.150 | 75.000 |
| 23. | Oltersdorf, Jutta | GER | 9.40 | 9.70 | 9.25 | 9.35 | 37.70 | 37.300 | 75.000 |
| 25. | Van Ravestijn, Jeannette | HOL | 9.45 | 9.55 | 9.10 | 9.50 | 37.60 | 37.100 | 74.700 |
| 26. | Kurbuweit, Petra | GER | 9.60 | 9.55 | 8.70 | 9.50 | 37.35 | 37.300 | 74.650 |
| 27. | Kelsall, Karen | CAN | 9.00 | 9.60 | 9.25 | 9.60 | 37.45 | 37.175 | 74.625 |
| 28. | Yaneva, Galia | BUL | 9.50 | 9.45 | 9.35 | 9.35 | 37.65 | 36.875 | 74.525 |
| 29. | Rope, Patti | CAN | 9.35 | 9.55 | 9.15 | 9.50 | 37.55 | 36.950 | 74.500 |
| 30. | Okazaki, Satoko | JPN | 8.95 | 9.60 | 8.70 | 9.55 | 36.80 | 37.650 | 74.450 |
| 31. | Kostova, Nina | BUL | 9.55 | 9.10 | 8.90 | 9.50 | 37.05 | 37.300 | 74.350 |
| 32. | De Keukeleire, Joelle | BEL | 9.50 | 9.40 | 9.20 | 9.40 | 37.50 | 36.600 | 74.100 |
| 33. | McDonnell, Nancy | CAN | 9.35 | 9.50 | 7.75 | 9.50 | 37.10 | 36.950 | 74.050 |
| 34. | Yamazaki, Nobue | JPN | 9.40 | 9.50 | 8.75 | 9.35 | 37.00 | 36.925 | 73.925 |
| 35. | Lennox, Avril | GBR | 9.40 | 9.60 | 9.15 | 8.90 | 37.05 | 36.825 | 73.875 |
| 36. | Bolleboom, Monique | HOL | 9.20 | 9.55 | 8.65 | 9.40 | .36.80 | 36.550 | 73.350 |

#### Men

| | | | FX | PH | R | V | PB | HB | AA Total | Prelim Total | FINAL TOTAL |
|---|---|---|---|---|---|---|---|---|---|---|---|
| 1. | Andrianov, Nikolai | URS | 9.80 | 9.70 | 9.75 | 9.80 | 9.65 | 9.70 | 58.40 | 58.250 | 116.650 |
| 2. | Kato, Sawao | JPN | 9.60 | 9.60 | 9.45 | 9.55 | 9.70 | 9.80 | 57.70 | 57.950 | 115.650 |
| 3. | Tsukahara, Mitsuo | JPN | 9.50 | 9.60 | 9.40 | 9.80 | 9.70 | 9.70 | 57.70 | 57.875 | 115.575 |
| 4. | Ditiatin, Alexandr | URS | 9.70 | 9.70 | 9.75 | 9.75 | 9.60 | 9.45 | 57.95 | 57.575 | 115.525 |
| 5. | Kajjiyama, Hiroshi | JPN | 9.60 | 9.65 | 9.65 | 9.65 | 9.65 | 9.60 | 57.80 | 57.625 | 115.425 |
| 6. | Szajna, Andrzej | POL | 9.60 | 9.60 | 9.60 | 9.80 | 9.55 | 9.55 | 57.70 | 56.925 | 114.625 |
| 7. | Nikolay, Michael | GDR | 9.30 | 9.85 | 9.45 | 9.60 | 9.35 | 9.60 | 57.15 | 56.450 | 113.600 |
| 8. | Molnar, Imre | HUN | 9.20 | 9.70 | 9.25 | 9.65 | 9.50 | 9.45 | 56.75 | 56.825 | 113.575 |
| 9. | Magyar, Zoltan | HUN | 9.45 | 9.90 | 8.95 | 9.20 | 9.25 | 9.55 | 56.30 | 57.125 | 113.425 |
| 10. | Jaeger, Bernd | GDR | 9.15 | 9.55 | 9.50 | 9.55 | 9.45 | 9.65 | 56.85 | 56.475 | 113.325 |
| 11. | Mack, Lutz | GDR | 9.20 | 9.45 | 9.50 | 9.55 | 9.40 | 9.55 | 56.65 | 56.500 | 113.150 |
| 12. | Young, Wayne | USA | 9.55 | 9.55 | 9.60 | 9.55 | 9.45 | 9.55 | 57.25 | 55.775 | 113.025 |
| 13. | Donath, Ferenc | HUN | 9.15 | 9.60 | 9.50 | 9.35 | 8.95 | 9.20 | 55.95 | 56.800 | 112.750 |
| 14. | Bretscher, Robert | SUI | 9.30 | 9.35 | 9.45 | 9.60 | 9.25 | 9.55 | 56.50 | 56.175 | 112.675 |
| 15. | Kormann, Peter | USA | 9.65 | 9.30 | 9.50 | 9.60 | 9.45 | 9.60 | 57.10 | 55.375 | 112.475 |
| 16. | Gienger, Eberhard | GER | 9.25 | 8.85 | 9.40 | 9.15 | 9.20 | 9.70 | 55.55 | 56.650 | 112.200 |
| 17. | Jorek, Edgar | GER | 9.45 | 9.45 | 9.40 | 9.15 | 9.45 | 9.25 | 56.15 | 55.625 | 111.775 |
| 18. | Tannenberger, Gustav | TCH | 9.40 | 9.45 | 9.30 | 9.50 | 9.40 | 9.50 | 56.55 | 55.200 | 111.750 |
| 19. | Rohrwick, Volker | GER | 9.40 | 9.50 | 9.10 | 9.50 | 9.30 | 8.65 | 55.45 | 56.100 | 111.550 |
| 20. | Tabak, Jiri | TCH | 9.60 | 9.20 | 9.15 | 9.70 | 9.40 | 9.55 | 56.60 | 54.700 | 111.300 |
| 21. | Thomas, Kurt | USA | 9.20 | 9.30 | 9.40 | 9.10 | 9.05 | 9.60 | 55.65 | 55.525 | 111.175 |
| 22. | Delesalle, Philip | CAN | 9.30 | 9.65 | 9.35 | 9.50 | 9.30 | 9.15 | 56.25 | 54.500 | 110.750 |
| 23. | Boerio, Henri | FRA | 9.10 | 8.60 | 9.55 | 9.10 | 8.70 | 9.00 | 54.05 | 56.450 | 110.500 |
| 24. | Carter, Keith | CAN | 9.15 | 9.30 | 9.30 | 9.35 | 9.25 | 9.30 | 55.65 | 54.650 | 110.300 |
| 25. | Netusil, Miloslav | TCH | 8.75 | 9.40 | 9.45 | 9.50 | 9.40 | 8.85 | 55.35 | 54.875 | 110.225 |
| 26. | Milanetto, Maurizio | ITA | 9.00 | 9.35 | 9.55 | 9.50 | 8.95 | 9.15 | 55.60 | 54.475 | 110.075 |
| 27. | Bachmann, Ueli | SUI | 9.00 | 9.35 | 9.00 | 9.45 | 8.90 | 9.50 | 55.20 | 54.800 | 110.000 |
| 27. | Gaille, Philippe | SUI | 8.85 | 9.45 | 9.30 | 9.15 | 9.10 | 9.45 | 55.30 | 54.700 | 110.000 |
| 29. | Oprescu, Nicolae | ROM | 9.05 | 8.20 | 9.35 | 9.50 | 9.25 | 9.40 | 54.75 | 55.150 | 109.900 |
| 30. | Koloko, Eric | FRA | 9.00 | 9.45 | 9.05 | 9.35 | 9.30 | 9.50 | 55.65 | 54.125 | 109.775 |
| 31. | Montesi, Maurizio | ITA | 9.20 | 9.40 | 9.45 | 9.60 | 8.85 | 9.20 | 55.70 | 54.050 | 109.750 |
| 32. | Cepoi, Sorin | ROM | 9.00 | 9.35 | 9.45 | 9.65 | 7.65 | 9.45 | 54.55 | 54.975 | 109.525 |
| 33. | Moy, Willi | FRA | 9.15 | 8.80 | 9.10 | 9.45 | 8.90 | 9.55 | 54.75 | 54.750 | 109.500 |
| 34. | Markelov, Vladimir | URS | 0.00 | 9.45 | 8.90 | 0.00 | 8.90 | 9.65 | 36.90 | 57.700 | 94.600 |
| 35. | Leclerc, Pierre | CAN | 1.00 | 0.00 | 0.00 | 0.00 | 9.05 | 9.35 | 19.40 | 54.350 | 73.750 |
| 36. | Grecu, Danut | ROM | 3.00 | 0.40 | 0.00 | 0.00 | 0.00 | 0.00 | .3.40 | 57.050 | 60.450 |

### Table C

#### Women

| | | Coun. | Prelim. | Final | Total |
|---|---|---|---|---|---|
| **VAULT** | | | | | |
| 1. | Kim, Nelli | URS | 9.850 | 9.95 | 19.800 |
| 2. | Tourischeva, Ludmilla | URS | 9.800 | 9.85 | 19.650 |
| 2. | Dombeck, Carola | GDR | 9.750 | 9.90 | 19.650 |
| 4. | Comaneci, Nadia | ROM | 9.775 | 9.85 | 19.625 |
| 5. | Escher, Gitta | GDR | 9.750 | 9.80 | 19.550 |
| 6. | Egervari, Marta | HUN | 9.700 | 9.75 | 19.450 |
| **UNEVEN PARALLEL BARS** | | | | | |
| 1. | Comaneci, Nadia | ROM | 10.000 | 10.00 | 20.000 |
| 2. | Ungureanu, Teodora | ROM | 9.900 | 9.90 | 19.800 |
| 3. | Egervari, Marta | HUN | 9.875 | 9.90 | 19.775 |
| 4. | Kische, Marion | GDR | 9.900 | 9.85 | 19.750 |
| 5. | Korbut, Olga | URS | 9.900 | 9.40 | 19.300 |
| 6. | Kim, Nelli | URS | 9.825 | 9.40 | 19.225 |
| **BEAM** | | | | | |
| 1. | Comaneci, Nadia | ROM | 9.950 | 10.00 | 19.950 |
| 2. | Korbut, Olga | URS | 9.825 | 9.90 | 19.725 |
| 3. | Ungureanu, Teodora | ROM | 9.800 | 9.90 | 19.700 |
| 4. | Tourischeva, Ludmilla | URS | 9.625 | 9.85 | 19.475 |
| 5. | Hellmann, Angelika | GDR | 9.550 | 9.90 | 19.450 |
| 6. | Escher, Gitta | GDR | 9.575 | 9.70 | 19.275 |
| **FLOOR EXERCISE** | | | | | |
| 1. | Kim, Nelli | URS | 9.850 | 10.00 | 19.850 |
| 2. | Tourischeva, Ludmilla | URS | 9.925 | 9.90 | 19.825 |
| 3. | Comaneci, Nadia | ROM | 9.800 | 9.95 | 19.750 |
| 4. | Pohludkova, Anna | TCH | 9.725 | 9.85 | 19.575 |
| 5. | Kische, Marion | GDR | 9.675 | 9.80 | 19.475 |
| 6. | Escher, Gitta | GDR | 9.700 | 9.75 | 19.450 |

#### Men

| | | | Prelim | Final | Total |
|---|---|---|---|---|---|
| **PARALLEL BARS** | | | | | |
| 1. | Kato, Sawao | JPN | 9.775 | 9.90 | 19.675 |
| 2. | Andrianov, Nikolai | URS | 9.750 | 9.75 | 19.500 |
| 3. | Tsukahara, Mitsuo | JPN | 9.675 | 9.80 | 19.475 |
| 4. | Jaeger, Bernd | GDR | 9.600 | 9.60 | 19.200 |
| 5. | Netusil, Miloslav | TCH | 9.525 | 9.60 | 19.125 |
| 6. | Szajna, Andrzej | POL | 9.500 | 9.45 | 18.950 |
| **HORIZONTAL BAR** | | | | | |
| 1. | Tsukahara, Mitsuo | JPN | 9.825 | 9.85 | 19.675 |
| 2. | Kenmotsu, Eizo | JPN | 9.750 | 9.75 | 19.500 |
| 3. | Gienger, Eberhard | GER | 9.675 | 9.80 | 19.475 |
| 3. | Boerio, Henri | FRA | 9.675 | 9.80 | 19.475 |
| 5. | Kryssin, Gennadi | URS | 9.650 | 9.60 | 19.250 |
| 6. | Donath, Ferenc | HUN | 9.600 | 9.60 | 19.200 |
| **FLOOR EXERCISE** | | | | | |
| 1. | Andrianov, Nikolai | URS | 9.650 | 9.80 | 19.450 |
| 2. | Marchenko, Vladimir | URS | 9.675 | 9.75 | 19.425 |
| 3. | Kormann, Peter | USA | 9.500 | 9.80 | 19.300 |
| 4. | Bruckner, Roland | GDR | 9.525 | 9.75 | 19.275 |
| 5. | Kato, Sawao | JPN | 9.600 | 9.65 | 19.250 |
| 6. | Kenmotsu, Eizo | JPN | 9.550 | 9.55 | 19.100 |
| **POMMEL HORSE** | | | | | |
| 1. | Magyar, Zoltan | HUN | 9.800 | 9.90 | 19.700 |
| 2. | Kenmotsu, Eizo | JPN | 9.775 | 9.80 | 19.575 |
| 3. | Andrianov, Nikolai | URS | 9.725 | 9.80 | 19.525 |
| 3. | Nikolay, Michael | GDR | 9.725 | 9.80 | 19.525 |
| 5. | Kato, Sawao | JPN | 9.700 | 9.70 | 19.400 |
| 6. | Ditiatin, Alexandr | URS | 9.650 | 9.70 | 19.350 |

#### (RINGS)

| | | | | | |
|---|---|---|---|---|---|
| **RINGS** | | | | | |
| 1. | Andrianov, Nikolai | URS | 9.850 | 9.80 | 19.650 |
| 2. | Ditiatin, Alexandr | URS | 9.750 | 9.80 | 19.550 |
| 3. | Grecu, Danut | ROM | 9.750 | 9.75 | 19.500 |
| 4. | Donath, Ferenc | HUN | 9.650 | 9.55 | 19.200 |
| 5. | Kenmotsu, Eizo | JPN | 9.625 | 9.55 | 19.175 |
| 6. | Kato, Sawao | JPN | 9.625 | 9.50 | 19.125 |
| **VAULT** | | | | | |
| 1. | Andrianov, Nikolai | URS | 9.675 | 9.775 | 19.450 |
| 2. | Tsukahara, Mitsuo | JPN | 9.650 | 9.725 | 19.375 |
| 3. | Kajiyama, Hiroshi | JPN | 9.675 | 9.600 | 19.275 |
| 4. | Grecu, Danut | ROM | 9.650 | 9.550 | 19.200 |
| 5. | Magyar, Zoltan | HUN | 9.575 | 9.575 | 19.150 |
| 5. | Molnar, Imre | HUN | 9.725 | 9.425 | 19.150 |

Often national and international champions, who are usually those with a reasonably good mark at every piece, do not win gold medals for all these events. The scores below show that Nadia Comaneci, who had the highest score in Competition 1 and became the Olympic Champion through winning Competition 2, took fourth place in the vaulting finals and third place in floor exercises. The World Champion Tourischeva did not even get into the finals on the bars.

In Competition 3 there are a possible 10 points in each apparatus event, to be added to half the apparatus score in Competition 1 (maximum 20 points).

Table C opposite shows that, to become the Olympic Vaulting Champion, Nelli Kim got 9.850 (that is the average of 9.80 and 9.90) in Competition 1 plus 9.95 in Competition 3, making a final winning score of 19.800.

The Soviet Union's women's team (left to right, Saadi, Tourischeva, Kim, Grozdova, Korbut, Filatova) standing to receive acclaim on becoming the winners at Montreal in 1976. They are flanked by the Rumanians and the East Germans in 2nd and 3rd places.

## Scoring in Women's Gymnastics

The present system of scoring in both men's and women's gymnastics dates back to the Olympic Games in London in 1948. Up to this time individual countries had used their own systems, but the London Olympiad brought dissatisfaction to a head among the competing nations and afterwards the F.I.G. technical committee produced a Code of Points which became the universal marking system.

In women's gymnastics, there are four pieces of apparatus with a voluntary and compulsory exercise on each in major competitions.

*Voluntary exercises* are marked out of 10 allocated as follows:

1 *Difficulty 3.00*
An exercise must have at least seven of the difficulties listed in the Code of Points, and at least three must be of superior rating. For every superior missing 0.6 is deducted, and for every medium missing 0.3 is deducted.
2 *Originality and Value of Connections 1.5*
An inexperienced gymnast lacks variety of linkages, while top gymnasts connect difficulties in original, interesting and daring ways. Gymnasts performing exceptional feats such as Nadia Comaneci, Nelli Kim and others are given credit here.
3 *Composition 0.5*
This is for the variety of moves, speed and direction, and the way in which the exercise is constructed.
4 *Execution and Amplitude 4.00*
This refers to the way the exercise is performed.
5 *General Impression 1.0*
Here the exercise is considered for overall impression.

*Compulsory exercises* are evaluated from 0 to 10 points in tenths of a point, and are judged for precision, correctness, rhythm and coordination. In women's gymnastics there are only two degrees of difficulty—medium and superior. If a superior or medium difficulty is omitted, 0.6 or 0.3 are deducted respectively

*Opposite:* Karin Janz, a member of the East German Olympic team, in a cartwheel in the vault.

Nadia Comaneci may well smile with the audience as she balances on her toes before a scoreboard that is incapable of showing correctly the 10 she obtained for her bars exercise at the Montreal Olympics.

but when a minor move is missing or altered the deduction is 0.1 or 0.2.

In major competitions and championships, a jury consisting of a superior judge and four judges sits at every piece of apparatus. In competitions between two nations, the superior judge is neutral and each country is represented by two judges. After every gymnast's performance, the judges send their marks to the superior judge, who disregards the highest and lowest marks and averages the middle two to give the score which appears on the electronic score board. The differences between the two middle scores, however, may not exceed

0.3 when the average is 9.50–10.0
0.5 when the average is 8.50–9.45
1.0 in all other cases

(During apparatus finals the limit is even tighter—0.2, 0.3 and 0.5.)

If the difference in scores exceeds the limits quoted above, the superior judge calls together the two judges concerned for a reconsideration of their valuation. He can substitute the base mark (the average between the mark he has given and the average received by the gymnast) if he cannot get the judges to change their marks. The superior judge's mark is used only in a dispute.

Differing interpretations of the code, or national bias, can often lead to incidents in international competitions. Regrettably groups of countries 'help' each other so that sometimes the best gymnasts or teams do not come out on top. Unfortunately the International Committee have not yet found a foolproof method of preventing this. They do have the power to send a judge off the floor but this is not done very often. One way would be to record every exercise on video-tape, but this would be slow and cumbersome.

The recognized names in the gymnastics world are often given more marks than they deserve and win competitions purely on name. Audiences are often extremely knowledgeable and make their sentiments felt. In Dortmund in 1962 a competition was held up for an hour when an American, Doris Fuchs, performed an exercise on the bars which was far before its time in originality and difficulty. She was not given her deserved mark so the audience booed and whistled.

At the Montreal Olympics, two gymnasts, Kim and Comaneci, received the full mark of 10. A 10 does not necessarily mean that a gymnast is perfect, although in the compulsory exercise she might well be. Comaneci on bars really was fantastic, and a 10 may merely show that the gymnast is much better than all her rivals. In fact, in Montreal Comaneci should sometimes have been given 20 out of 10 to correspond to the very high marks undeservedly given other competitors, as the difference in scores did not reflect the difference in quality of the exercises. When marking, a judge compares the moves he sees to the picture of the ideal in his mind. Marks from one competition should not be compared with those of another marked in different circumstances and by different judges.

With the emergence of so many great gymnasts lately, the Code, in its present form, is proving inadequate, and changes are being discussed. It is revised every four years and there is a move afoot to have only neutral judges at finals.

One change needed is to award credit for R.O.V. (risk, originality and virtuosity), as appears in the men's code, so that new and risky moves would be rewarded with high marks. However, there are two sides to this coin as one does not wish gymnastics to become merely a sport of daring stunts. Some countries such as the Soviet Union are already amending the Code for their own national championships, grading their difficulties and giving extra credit for 'superior superior' difficulties.

At the European Championships in Prague in 1977, there was a case for some sort of amendment to the Code. The Soviet Union's Nelli Kim did two extremely difficult and original vaults, the full twisting Tsukahara (half-turn on and one-and-a-half twisting somersaults off) and a straight-bodied Tsukahara (half-turn on and one-and-a-half straight somersaults off), while Comaneci did a tucked and piked Tsukahara. Kim did her vaults well but with slight mistakes. Comaneci did the easier vaults with her usual impeccable form. Which of the two girls should win, the one with the more difficult vaults or the one with the better performance?

Andrea Bieger of West Germany at the chalk bin— a crucial moment for the gymnast.

# Scoring in Men's Gymnastics

Men must perform voluntary and compulsory exercises on six pieces of apparatus. Ten points (in tenths of a point) are at stake for the perfect exercise and, in *voluntary exercises*, they are allocated as follows for three separate elements:

| | |
|---|---|
| Difficulty | 3.4 |
| Execution | 4.4 |
| Combination | 1.6 |
| | Total: 9.4 |

There are also three bonus factors, risk—0.2, originality—0.2 and virtuosity—0.2 (known as R.O.V.), thus bringing the total up to ten.

As explained in detail on pages 19-23, there are three competitions in championships—Competition 1, the Team Competition; Competition 2, the Individual All Around Finals; and Competition 3, the Individual Event Finals. We saw how these competitions relate to one another in terms of an individual gymnast's performance.

As regards the content of the gymnastic exercises for men, all three competitions have slightly different requirements. This mainly concerns difficulty, which is divided into three types.

| | | |
|---|---|---|
| A parts | (basic elements or combination) | 0.2 |
| B parts | (medium difficult elements or combination) | 0.4 |
| C parts | (superior difficult elements or combination) | 0.6 |

The figures are the maximum points to be deducted from the gymnast's score for omitting stipulated elements.

The stipulated number of A, B, and C parts in major competitions are:

| | A | B | C | | |
|---|---|---|---|---|---|
| Competition 1 | 4 | 5 | 1 | = | 3.4 |
| Competition 2 | 3 | 4 | 2 | = | 3.4 |
| Competition 3 | 2 | 3 | 3 | = | 3.4 |

The number of A, B and C parts totals 10 for Competition 1, 9 for Competition 2 and 8 for Competition 3. In fact to avoid penalty eleven parts or elements must be performed in every exercise. So the missing parts must be made up of elements valued at not less than A grade and, in practice, it is more common in Competition 3 to see them of B or even C grade.

The next sub-division of the whole exercise, execution (valued at 4.4), is really divided into two parts. First, the technical performance presented by the gymnast is considered and then the style of performance —are the legs together and the toes pointed and so on. Then 'combination' is taken into account (valued at 1.6), which assesses the skill with which the gymnast puts the various elements together.

Finally the remaining 0.6 is held in reserve to be added to the final score when the judges consider that certain elements involve any of the following: risk (danger to the gymnast or the exercise); originality (a new element or a new approach to an existing one); and virtuosity (above the normal technical requirement).

As in women's marking, the superior judge disregards the highest and lowest marks and averages the middle two. In men's gymnastics the difference between the two middle scores may not exceed

0.1 when the average is 9.60–10.00
0.2 when the average is 9.00–9.55
0.3 when the average is 8.00–8.95
0.5 when the average is 6.50–7.95
0.8 when the average is 4.00–6.45
1.0 in all other cases.

In *compulsory exercises* the combination and elements of difficulty are arranged in advance by the technical committee of the F.I.G. The distribution of marks is also different and the judges must consider only two main factors, interpretation of the published text which sets out what the compulsory exercises are, and execution with regard to style and technical competence. (The maximum mark awarded for these two is 9.8.) The gymnast can obtain the other 0.2 points by demonstrating virtuosity either in part or throughout the whole sequence.

A compulsory exercise will contain 3 to 4 B parts in addition to the necessary A parts. Omission of a part or sequence in a compul-

Werner Steinmetz of West Germany shows excellent form, performing an 'L' or half-lever on the still rings. The score in the background refers to a previous vault exercise.

sory exercise can bring about a more severe deduction than one would expect for a similar omission during a voluntary routine. The inclusion of an extra movement is treated with a deduction of 0.3 and, should the movement preceding or following it be made easier, a further 0.1–0.3 penalty is given.

When a compulsory exercise is performed in accordance with the published instructions, deductions for style and execution are the only penalties that can be made.

## The Art of Judging Gymnastics

As a competitive sport, gymnastics is akin to figure skating or diving. It is a demonstration sport where the competitor's success is assessed by the subjective judgement of officials who have a knowledge of the technical rules and regulations governing the competition. There is no contact with an opponent as there is in sports such as boxing or fencing, and consequently no knockout or touch of a foil to guide the judges. Four judges supervised by a superior judge evaluate and score each exercise. A judge is faced with a complex task in which the soundness of his knowledge and his skill in applying pre-determined rules is set against his ability to interpret those rules with his critical sense.

He must put his knowledge to proper use at the proper time without allowing himself to be influenced by any emotional interference that would make his work an instrument of partiality. However, the very subjective nature of a judge's work gives rise to two conflicting questions. Should the judge adopt a stereotyped approach, whereby he merely applies the rules and pays no heed to the world as it moves about him, or should he rather be a technician and a verifier, a man who is aware of his own environment and judges it, influenced by his surroundings and influencing them in his turn?

Although a judge must seek a common denominator for penalties, he must also appreciate the value of new ways of execution and interpretation. It is vital that his training should keep him technically abreast of all new developments. One of the greatest

Rainer Hanschke of East Germany performing on the pommelled horse, while Alexandr Dityatin (Soviet Union) concentrates on his floor exercise.

risks for a gymnast can be ignorance on the part of those who judge him.

A judgement may influence a gymnast's work and, therefore, the competition; but to a greater extent the gymnast's work, through the validity of his performance, will influence the judgements. These reciprocal influences ensure a continual up-dating of the marking code.

Only through a constant analysis and study of the evolution of techniques can a judge remain unswayed by the spectacular side of gymnastics and be able to concentrate on the elements of difficulty and the combination of movements. He will also be in a much better position to judge the most appropriate way of penalizing errors, and to recognize elements of risk, originality and virtuosity.

Disparities in assessment by the four judges frequently exist and often both the gymnast and the audience are dissatisfied and the competition is spoiled. Lengthy interruptions due to disputes sometimes lead to more unsatisfactory scores and put the success of the competition at risk.

The solution to the problem lies in two different directions. The superior judge should be the arbitrator, not only by directing the judges and intervening when there are disparities in their assessments, but also by including in his report for the F.I.G. a statistical statement of all the plus or minus errors of the four judges. This would give the F.I.G. a complete picture of the abilities of each judge and also act as an incentive for a judge to be concerned with his own errors.

Another means of overcoming the inherent problems of the judging panel is the use of video-tape or closed-circuit television. But these methods detract from the personal factor of emotional impressions which are still essential in evaluating a gymnast. Video is like putting a filter before the action. An art critic, for instance, looks at the original masterpiece, knowing that a photograph would be a poor substitute.

Clearly the video is of use to a judge who may be out of his depth in recognizing a new technique either because of its originality or because of the speed of execution, but mostly visual aids should be used only in the last resort, otherwise gymnasts will find themselves governed by machines.

# The Movements Introduction

In major gymnastics events, competitors are required to perform a sequence of compulsory exercises which are stipulated by the F.I.G. in the Code of Points and to add to these a series of optional movements. (The structure of competitions is described in detail on pages 19-31.) Space does not permit us to show every movement—indeed that would be impossible because new movements are continually being developed—so we have shown the ones which the spectator is most likely to see. What the printed page can never show is the speed and fluidity of these movements. The gymnast proceeds swiftly without pausing from one movement to another on a particular piece of apparatus.

In view of the general similarities between men's and women's floor exercises and vaults, the movements appear only in the women's section.

Before every piece of apparatus is worked there is a warm-up period of about three minutes. For two apparatus, the floor and the balance beam, there is a set time limit for each routine. The other pieces of apparatus are not timed but the gymnast knows that, to qualify for the maximum possible marks, he or she must show a stipulated number of elements of a certain difficulty, which must be tied together with linking movements. Once the elements required have been executed, nothing can be gained and much can be lost by protracting the exercise, so the gymnast performs the routine as expeditiously as possible without seeming to be in haste.

There is a set order for working the apparatus. For women gymnasts it is: vaulting, uneven parallel (asymmetric) bars, balance beam and the floor, for men it is the floor, pommelled horse, still rings, vaulting, parallel bars and horizontal bar. Often at major events the gymnasts are divided into groups and you will see all the apparatus being worked at once, for instance one women's group will be vaulting while another is at the bars and often the applause from spectators for one exercises will cut across another.

# Women's Movements **Vaulting**

The basic techniques of vaulting are common to both men and women. Both must develop an explosion of power—a combination of horizontal velocity and vertical thrust—to move over the horse. The vaults themselves are nowadays essentially the same, for since the late 1960s those performed by women have become increasingly difficult, rivalling men's in their complexity.

There are some differences however. Men vault down the length of the horse, using either end to obtain their elevating thrust. Women vault across the horse, placing their hands on the centre. Women are allowed two attempts and men only one. The men's horse is over 30 centimetres (1 foot) higher than the women's.

Each vault is divided into two sections —first and second flight. First flight lasts from the moment the gymnast starts the vault until the moment she touches the horse. Position and lift of the body, its path through the air and its position as it reaches the horse are the points to watch for here. The vault is completed in the second flight, in which balance, stretch of the body, descent and general direction must all be taken into account.

There are three kinds of vault—straight, in which the gymnast's body must be in a horizontal position as she passes over the horse; handspring, in which she must pass through a handstand on the horse; and those that involve turning around the horizontal axis—that is, somersaulting. In each type, the gymnast's hands must touch the horse.

Many of the more difficult vaults have only been developed in recent years, in particular by Olga Korbut and Nelli Kim. Indeed the last one shown had not by 1978 been performed in competition: a vault for the space-age, it will undoubtedly appear in the 1980s.

## Horizontal Vaults
### Hecht Vault

Even this, one of the simplest of the through vaults, has its problems. Keeping her body and legs straight all the time, the gymnast leaps onto the horse, keeping her body horizontal above it, and then propels herself forwards, landing with her back to the horse.

### Hecht with Full Turn

In this vault, rarely if ever attempted by women and in any case a strangely inelegant movement, the gymnast must complete a full turn in the air before landing again with her back to the horse.

# Handsprings

## Handspring

Keeping her body and legs straight all the time, the gymnast leaps onto the horse, passes through the handstand position to land with her back to the horse.

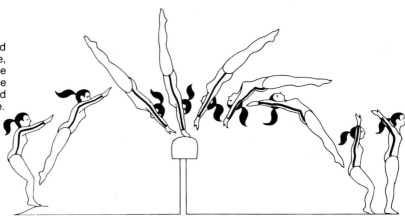

## Yamashita

For this vault the gymnast moves through the handstand and then, as she leaves the horse, goes forwards into the piked position before straightening her body and landing with her back to the horse.

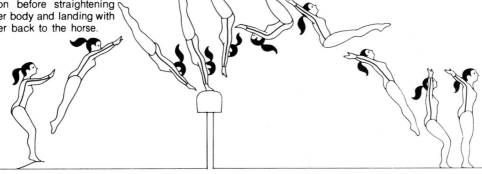

## Half Turn, Handspring, Half Turn

The gymnast dives towards the horse, executing a half turn as she does so. She reaches the horse in a handstand facing her starting direction. The vault is completed with a second half turn so that she lands with her back to the horse.

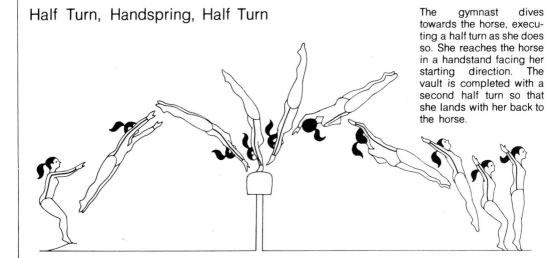

## Handspring and Full Turn

Having sprung onto the horse in a handstand, the gymnast completes the vault by executing a full turn to land with her back to the horse.

## Handspring and One-and-a-half Turn

For this vault, the gymnast is required to execute a one-and-a-half turn as she leaves the horse, having first moved through the handstand.

## Half Turn, Handspring and Full Turn

Diving, onto the horse, and executing a half turn as she does so, the gymnast moves through the handstand and then does a complete turn to land facing the horse.

# Somersaults

## Handspring, One-and-a-half Forward Tucked Somersault

Having sprung onto the horse in a handstand, the gymnast must complete her vault with a forward somersault (with body tucked), executed one-and-a-half times so that she lands with her back to the horse.

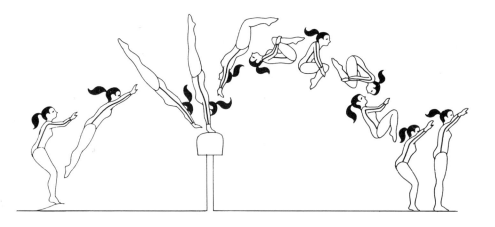

## One-and-a-half Forward Tucked Somersault, Handspring

The gymnast must execute a forward tucked somersault one-and-a-half times so that she lands on the horse in a handstand. She completes the vault with a handspring and lands with her back to the horse.

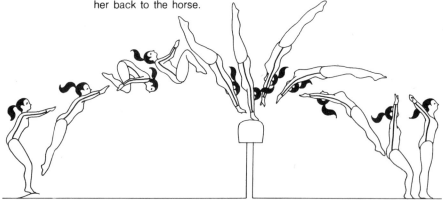

## Cartwheel, One- and-a-half Backward Piked Somersault (Tsukahara)

Cartwheeling through the air as she takes off, the gymnast must land on the horse sideways on, with one hand in front of the other. She then executes a backward somersault in the piked position to land facing the horse.

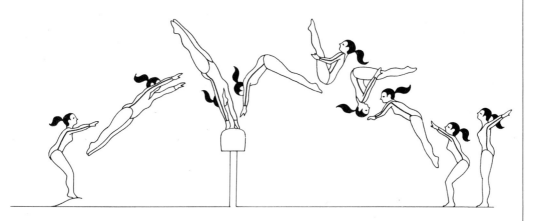

## One-and-a-half Forward Tucked Somersault, Handspring and One-and-a-half Forward Tucked Somersault

Having started with a forward somersault in the tucked position done one-and-a-half times so that she reaches the horse in a handstand, the gymnast must complete her vault by doing the same somersault yet again, finally landing with her back to the horse.

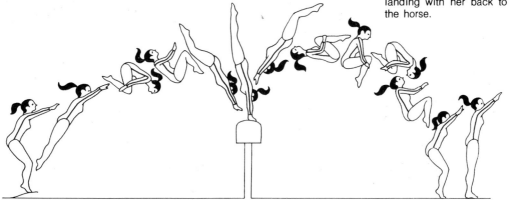

# Uneven Parallel (Asymmetric) Bars

It was in 1956 that movements on the high and low parallel (asymmetric) bars were first started. Before, women had used parallel bars in much the same way as men but, because of their build, with less success. The change was astounding. The two bars offered unlimited scope for creative ideas—for what men can do on one horizontal bar women can do in two different ways on their bars. Since then, this part of the gymnast's performance has attracted literally thousands (perhaps even millions) of girls to gymnastics.

Exercises on the bars must be continuous. Judges look in particular at the various hand grips the gymnast employs and at her swinging movements, suspension and the passage of her body between the bars.

## Mounts
### Jump to Hip Support

The gymnast jumps in the air, executes a 360 degree spin and, grasping the low bar, then circles over it forwards, down and up again, ending the movement in the front support position on the low bar. The spin itself is relatively easy—but it is not so easy to move smoothly on to the next part of the movement.

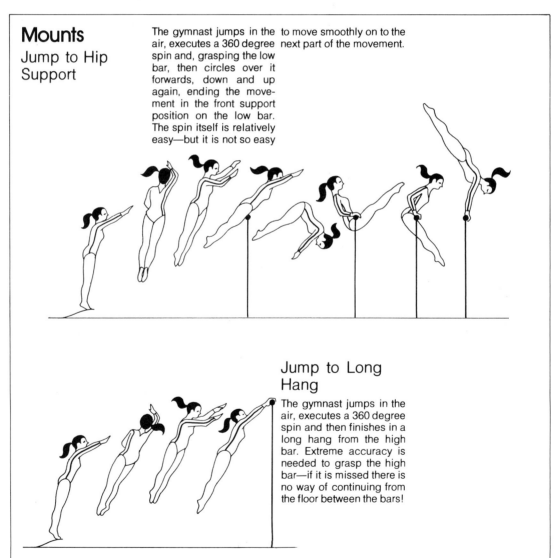

### Jump to Long Hang

The gymnast jumps in the air, executes a 360 degree spin and then finishes in a long hang from the high bar. Extreme accuracy is needed to grasp the high bar—if it is missed there is no way of continuing from the floor between the bars!

## Jump through Kip to Hang

The gymnast swings herself under the low bar and then hangs in the piked position from it. She then kips and catches the high bar, finishing in a hang.

## Jump to Pike Support

Jumping to the low bar, the gymnast momentarily supports herself above it, executes a half turn and brings her legs through to finish in a piked support on it.

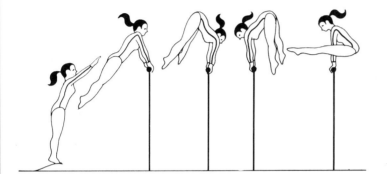

## Jump to Pike Hang

The gymnast jumps to the low bar, somersaults forwards over it, finally hanging from the high bar in a straddled pike position. Sufficient clearance as she passes over the low bar during the somersault is essential if she is to fold her body and catch the high bar.

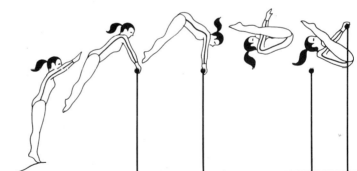

## Swings

## Back Support to Front Support

Supporting herself in front of the high bar, the gymnast must circle backwards, bringing her feet between her arms. Then, doing a three-quarters backwards circle, she releases the high bar and catches the low one in the front support position.

## Glide to Hang

Swinging back from the low bar, the gymnast passes her legs through her hands and continues to swing up over the low bar with sufficient velocity to project herself forwards to hang from the high bar.

## Back Support, Circle to Back Support

From a back support position on the high bar, the gymnast circles back up and through the piked position to finish once again in the back support position.

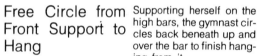

## Free Circle from Front Support to Hang

Supporting herself on the high bars, the gymnast circles back beneath up and over the bar to finish hanging from it.

## Free Hip Circle to Straddle Support

Supporting herself on the high bar, the gymnast first drops down, then does a full backwards circle and finishes by supporting herself on the high bar, legs straddling her arms.

## Back Seat Circle, Half Turn to Hang

From the back support on the high bar, the gymnast brings her legs up and then down to pass between her arms. Then, circling forwards, she releases her grip, twists and grasps the bar again, to finish hanging from it.

## Upstarts
### Half Turn to Hang

Hanging back from the low bar with arms straight, the gymnast moves her legs forward into a piked position, then propels herself through a 180-degree turn upwards to grasp the high bar and hangs down from it.

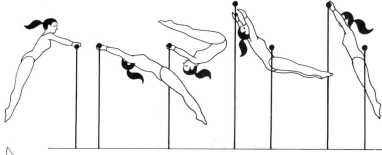

## Rear Lying Hang to Back Support

Hanging back from the high bar over the low bar, the gymnast passes her legs·through her hands and, obtaining as much height as possible, uses the resultant swing to return under the bar and end in the back support· position.

## Front Stand, Jump to Handstand

Standing on the low bar and grasping the high one, the gymnast jumps up to a handstand on the high bar.

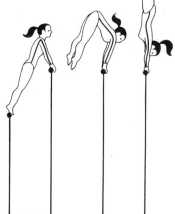

## Rear Lying Hang to Handstand

From a rear lying hang on the high bar, the gymnast brings her feet into the piked position, kips and brings her body back and up to a handstand on the high bar.

## Front Lying Hang to Handstand

From a front lying hang from the high bar (the hips in contact with the low bar), the gymnast swings back and up, releases the high bar and grasps the low one in a handstand.

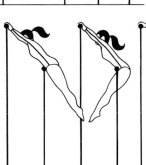

# Somersaults

## Radochla Somersault

From an inner front support position on the low bar, the gymnast swings her legs back and performs a forwards somersault, at the same time moving backwards to catch the high bar in a straddle, finishing in a hang.

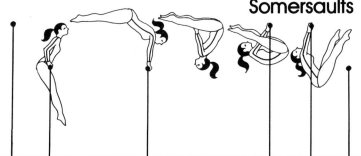

## Squat Stand to Rear Hang

Starting by squatting on the high bar, the gymnast must flick herself up and back so that she finishes by hanging from the high bar.

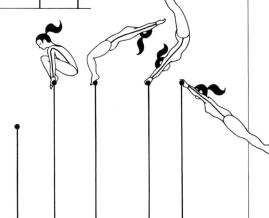

# Dismounts
## Hecht Dismount

Hanging back from the high bar, the gymnast swings forwards, folding her body round the lower bar and continuing to circle until her legs point down. At this point she extends her body and ends by jumping down to the floor.

## Handstand, Circle to Handstand, Backward Somersault Dismount

Circling up through a handstand on the high bar, the gymnast continues to swing down and then does a backwards somersault to land facing the bars.

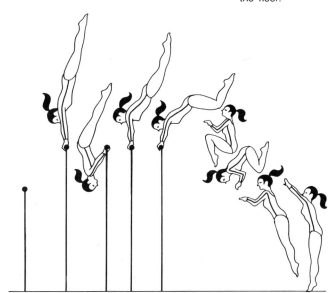

## Jump to Handstand, Straddle Dismount

Jumping up to a brief handstand on the high bar, the gymnast then lets go, swinging through a straddle to land with her back to the bars.

### Front Support to Rear Stand

Gripping the high bar, the gymnast moves up into the outer front support, then swings down and under the bar, twisting herself over the low bar to land with her back to the bars.

### Front Support, Hecht Dismount to Rear Stand

Supporting herself on the high bar, the gymnast moves to the front support position and swings legs down, under the bar and up. Then she circles back over the bar and executes a Hecht dismount over both bars.

### Front Support to Rear Stand

This movement is performed in the same way as the previous one, except that the gymnast must do a 360-degree twist as she dismounts.

# Balance Beam

The balance beam is a mere four inches wide. To perform the complex manoeuvres shown here on such a narrow space requires a fine sense of touch, body tension and an inner balance. Lean slightly to one side and an equal amount of body weight must be displaced to the other; keep the body too slack and too great a counter-lean will be necessary.

The gymnast must use the whole length of the beam and must do large and small turns, jumps and leaps, and running and walking steps, and also include displays of balance. Too many lying and sitting positions must be avoided.

Acrobatic exercises have become increasingly difficult since Olga Korbut first did a standing back somersault and F.I.G. officials considered banning the movement. Nowadays a competitor who fails to include such an exercise will not gain national status—let alone world recognition.

Today, as always, one slip from the beam may cost a competition or a career.

## Mounts

## Jump

The gymnast jumps from the springboard on to the end of the beam, landing on one foot, keeping the other free, at the same time extending her arms.

## Jump to Handstand

With a run up of 5 or 6 metres (about 6 yards), the gymnast springs high, placing her hands on the end of the beam and swinging up into a handstand. A half turn may also be included in the movement. Extreme body tension is required to do this successfully.

## Jump with Half Turn on One Leg

Doing a half turn as she jumps, the gymnast lands on the beam on one leg and stretches the other back, extending her arms at the same time.

## Jump to Back Support

Jumping onto the beam, the gymnast first squats on it and then hangs from it in back support.

## Jump to Split Sit

The gymnast jumps onto the beam and lands in the split position, facing to her front.

## Forward Somersault to Stand

Executing a front somersault as she jumps, the gymnast lands on the beam in a crouch and then straightens up.

## Leaps
### Stride Leap

The gymnast executes a stride leap, stretching one foot as far forwards as possible, the other as far back as possible, and lands with one foot outstretched behind her.

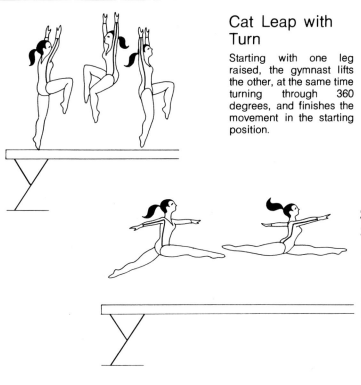

## Cat Leap with Turn

Starting with one leg raised, the gymnast lifts the other, at the same time turning through 360 degrees, and finishes the movement in the starting position.

## Stride Leap to Split Leap

Starting with a stride leap, the gymnast must then change the position of her legs (bringing the front one back and vice versa) into a split leap, landing on her left foot.

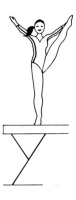

# Hold Positions
## Stand with One Leg Stretched

The gymnast stands sideways on the beam on one leg, holding the other in one hand and extending the other arm.

## Backward Scale

Stretching her head and trunk back and down as far as possible, the gymnast reaches the splits position, balancing on one leg and stretching the other as far as possible.

## Arabesque

Stretching far forwards with body and one arm in a straight line (the other arm stretched out for balance), the gymnast stretches both legs into the full splits position. Today most gymnasts perform this without touching the beam with either hand.

## Acrobatic Movements
### Forward Handspring

The gymnast steps forward into a handspring, completes it and then steps forward again.

### Flic-Flac (or Back Handspring)

The gymnast executes a flic-flac (or back handspring), finishing the movement with arms and head bent forwards.

### Aerial Walkover

In this movement the gymnast as it were walks over herself in the air. Balancing on one foot, leaning forwards and down and stretching the other foot up, she pushes off, keeping her body in the same position, and lands on her other leg, ready to step forwards.

### Backward Tucked Somersault

Standing with arms at her sides, the gymnast bends her knees slightly and springs vertically upwards. She thrusts her arms upward to help gain height. As she reaches maximum height, the gymnast drives her knees to her chest and rotates her body backwards, keeping a tucked position. When she sees where she is to land, she extends her legs and continues to raise her upper body until landing.

# Balancing Movements

## Forward Roll and Balance

The gymnast rolls forward on the beam to finish in a crouching position on one leg, with arms and the other leg outstretched.

## Backward Roll

This movement must be performed without using the hands and with the hips at a slight angle to the beam. The gymnast rolls backwards, keeping one arm on each side of the beam, and finishes in a kneeling position, with head and arms bent forwards.

## Balance Sit and Forward Roll

Starting in a balance sit, in which her legs are stretched up and her arms out, her bottom providing the only support, she swings her legs down and then up to roll forwards, supporting herself on her hands. She finishes the movement sitting on the beam, with one foot on it, stretching her arms and the other leg out.

## Side Handstand and Split

The gymnast kicks sideways and up to reach a side handstand, then she lowers her legs to finish in the splits position sideways on, with arms outstretched.

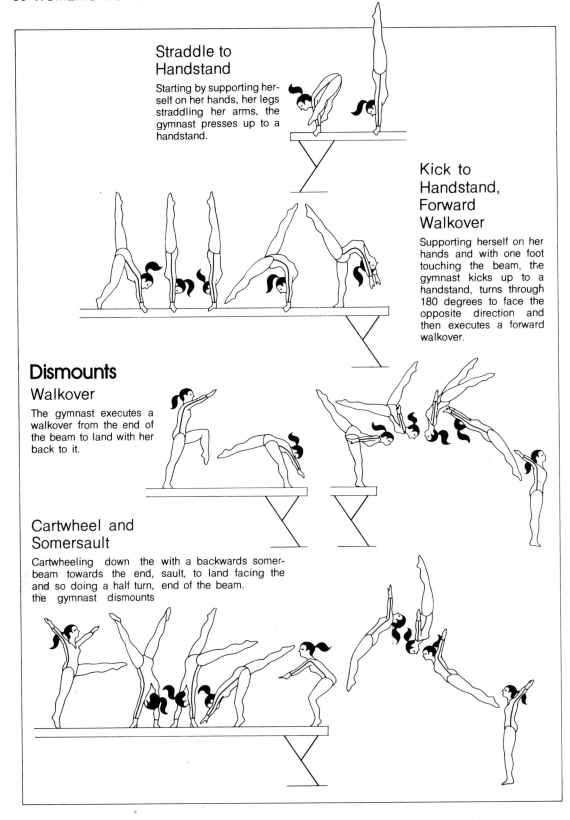

## Straddle to Handstand

Starting by supporting herself on her hands, her legs straddling her arms, the gymnast presses up to a handstand.

## Kick to Handstand, Forward Walkover

Supporting herself on her hands and with one foot touching the beam, the gymnast kicks up to a handstand, turns through 180 degrees to face the opposite direction and then executes a forward walkover.

# Dismounts

## Walkover

The gymnast executes a walkover from the end of the beam to land with her back to it.

## Cartwheel and Somersault

Cartwheeling down the beam towards the end, and so doing a half turn, the gymnast dismounts with a backwards somersault, to land facing the end of the beam.

# Floorwork

Of all the different women's exercises, those done on the floor show off the elegance and beauty of the female form to the greatest advantage. A top performer's combination of a superbly functional body with artistic and gymnastic talent can lead to a display of stunning visual and athletic appeal.

Acrobatic movements on the floor—somersaults, handstands, flic-flacs, handsprings and so on—are linked together with tumbles, jumps, pirouettes, spins and other dance-related movements, as the gymnast covers the entire floor area during her routine, which must last no longer than 1 minute 30 seconds.

The exercise is accompanied by piano music and some countries have pianists specially trained for this type of accompaniment.

In contrast to these dance-like routines, men perform the acrobatic movements without musical accompaniment and the performance appears altogether more vigorous and masculine. Balance, hold and strength accordingly are important in men's floor exercises, while in the women's the emphasis is on flexibility and expressiveness, making this event the most popular of all, judging by the often ecstatic applause of the audience.

## Springs
### Neck Spring and Turn

Lying with her shoulders on the floor and body and legs bent back, the gymnast first stands on her hands, then twists herself through 180 degrees and finishes by supporting herself on her hands. This is one of the countless variations based on the kip or upstart.

## Neck Spring to Piked Sit

Lying with her shoulders on the floor and body and legs bent back, the gymnast springs forward and up to land in a deep pike, with head, arms and body bent forwards.

## Body Wave
### Forward Body Wave

With knees bent, and head, arms and body leaning forwards and down, the gymnast first brings her body and arms to vertical, then circles her arms backwards and bends her body and head as far back as possible to reverse the starting position, and finishes with body straight and arms outstretched.

# Leaps, Jumps and Rolls

### Stag Leap

The gymnast takes off on one foot and bends the other leg at the knee. While in the air, she must keep her leg bent, lifting the knee as far forwards as possible, and stretch the other leg back, finally landing on one foot.

## Arch Jump

The gymnast jumps in the air from both feet, throwing her arms up and arching her back as far as possible. There are different variations of arch jumps, with different leg positions.

### Tour Jeté

Starting with arms raised and one leg extended, the gymnast must execute a 180-degree turn, landing in the starting position but facing the opposite direction and with the other leg raised.

## Tinsicas

Tinsicas involve the gymnast in walking on all four limbs. She leans towards the floor and pushes off with one leg. Her hands touch the floor one after another. As her first hand leaves the floor, her first foot touches it. She pushes off from the floor with her second hand, lifting and arching her body, and comes to the vertical, stretching her second leg out to maintain balance. Finally she returns to the starting position.

## Aerial Cartwheel

Taking off on one foot, the gymnast cartwheels through 180 degrees to land on one foot again, facing the opposite direction.

## Forward Roll

After a short run, the gymnast dives forwards into a roll, keeping her body straight throughout the flight.

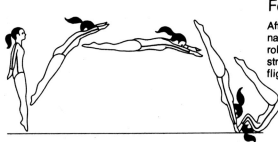

## Backward Jump and Forward Roll

Keeping her body straight, the gymnast must jump backwards into a 180-degree turn and then execute a forward dive and roll.

## Backward Roll and Handstand

Rolling backwards, the gymnast raises herself to a handstand and then turns through 180 degrees.

## Aerial Forward Walkover

With arms outstretched and one leg bent, the gymnast bends over so that her head, body and legs form a straight line. Then, gaining impetus from the lower leg, she twists through 360 degrees in the air, landing on one foot, with one leg outstretched and head, arms and body thrown back.

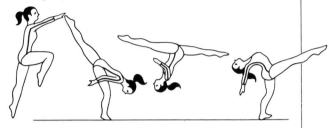

# Flexing and Bending

## Backward Walkover to Squat

Starting with head and arms thrown back and one foot outstretched, the gymnast walks backwards on her hands, passing through a handstand and lowering herself to a seated position on the floor.

## Flic-Flacs

With hands outstretched, the gymnast leaps forward on one foot, turning through 180 degrees. She then circles backwards onto her hands, using the momentum to thrust off again to perform several flic-flacs in succession. As it is easier for a man to do this than for a woman, the exercise is placed in the easy category for men and in the difficult category for women.

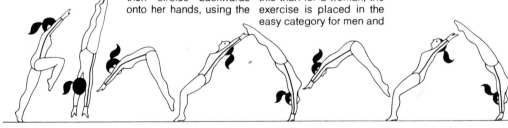

## One-Leg Flic-Flac

Here the gymnast thrusts off from only one leg.

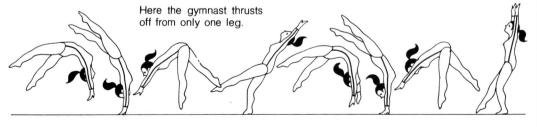

## Cartwheel and Flic-Flac from One Leg

Starting with a cartwheel, the gymnast swings straight into a one-leg flic-flac.

## Flic-Flac to Splits

Jumping back onto her hands as if she were starting a flic-flac, the gymnast then snaps her forward leg through her hands to land seated in the splits position.

## Flic-Flac to Sit

After a flic-flac onto her hands, the gymnast twists herself through 180 degrees to land on the floor in the piked position, facing in the opposite direction from which she started.

## Flic-Flac and Tucked Somersault

After executing a flic-flac, the gymnast does a backward tucked somersault.

# Somersaults

## Forward Somersault

The gymnast jumps forwards into a tucked somersault and lands facing the same direction. This is more difficult for women than men.

## Jump and Forward Stretched Somersault

Jumping backwards and turning through 180 degrees, the gymnast then executes a forward stretched somersault, landing on one foot with head, body and arms thrown back, and extending the other leg.

## Backward Somersault

Starting from a handstand, the gymnast flips down, forwards and up so that she is standing straight with arms outstretched. She then does a tucked backwards somersault.

## Backward Stretched Somersault

First cartwheeling from one leg through 180 degrees, the gymnast then does a stretched backward somersault through 360, 540 or 720 degrees or even more.

## Backward Stretched Somersault with Step Out

Cartwheeling from one leg through 180 degrees, the gymnast then executes a stretched backward somersault, at the same time extending her legs as far apart from each other as possible.

# Men's Movements **Pommelled Horse**

Once sat on, jumped on, kicked and generally ill-treated, the pommelled horse has today come up in the world and is scarcely touched at all. Adorned with a head and a tail when it was used as an aid to improving horsemanship, it has now shed these life-like reminders of its original role and is left with a neck (on the gymnast's left) and a rump (on his right), plus two handles screwed into its body.

Competitors must use all parts of the horse and must include circles with one leg— known for obvious reasons as shears—and with both. The dismount must be in line with the overall difficulty of the routine and the gymnast must also include some of the movements classed as especially difficult. Shown here too is one new movement, 'the flourish or windmill', developed in preparation for the 1980 Olympic Games.

## Shears
### Front Shears

This is the most familiar movement performed on the pommelled horse. The gymnast swings over the horse from side to side with legs apart, changing the position of his legs while straddling the horse. If his right leg is forwards and he swings to the right, the shears are termed 'forwards', that is, in the direction the hips are leaning.

### Back Shears

This action—in which, as in the front shears, the gymnast moves from one side of the horse to the other—is performed away from the inclination of the hips, hence the term 'back shears'. Much more skill and strength is required.

### Back Shears with Turn

In this movement, the gymnast supports himself first on his right hand, then on his left, as he moves from one side of the horse to the other. It is by no means simple to keep this routine rhythmic and elegant.

# Circles of Both Legs Together
## Double Circles in the Saddle

Grasping the handles, the gymnast circles over the horse, keeping his legs straight and supporting himself first on both hands, then on his right and finally on his left (or vice versa). His body must not touch the saddle (the area of the horse between the handles). This is a basic element in constructing a competitive routine.

Side view

The front view of the double circle in the saddle shows that the gymnast must displace his shoulders to the right while he swings his legs over the horse to the left. The reverse happens in the second half of the movement. Points are deducted if he opens or bends his legs.

Front view

## Double Circles on End

Placing his hands on the end of the horse, the gymnast circles over it, keeping his legs straight all the time. He must displace his shoulders to the right as he swings to the left and vice versa. This is a difficult movement: the handles impede the legs and the hands have only a narrow area in which to operate.

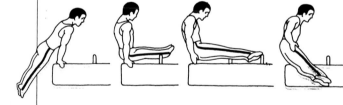

## Dismounts

The three basic actions used in dismounting at the end of a routine are the flank, front and rear vaults.

## Flank Vault

Placing both hands on the end of the horse, the gymnast swings up onto his right hand and, bending at the waist and keeping his legs straight, vaults over the horse to land with his back to it.

## Front Vault

Characteristic of this movement is the high flourish with the legs at the end of the vault. Keeping his legs straight, the gymnast vaults over the horse, balancing on one hand and extending the other arm, and lands by the end of the horse.

## Rear Vault

To execute a rear vault, the gymnast must swing the back of his legs over the horse once, keeping them straight and balancing on one hand. For a double rear vault (shown here) his legs must pass over the horse twice, for a triple, three times.

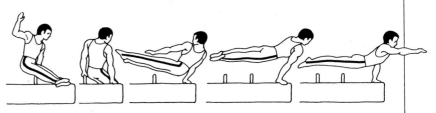

## Combination of the Three Basic Movements

This combination of vaults would form about two tenths of a gymnast's routine which will last 30 to 40 seconds. The gymnast starts with a flank vault, moves into a front vault and completes the sequence with a double rear vault.

## Difficult Movements
### End Work

Movements confined to the end of the horse require a great deal of skill and practice. The handles must be negotiated without breaking swing and rhythm. The performer's hands, which must support the weight of his body, are restricted to a narrow base. Since they are often at an acute angle his wrists must be particularly strong and supple. The gymnast must balance on one hand at the end of the horse and, keeping his legs straight, sweep them over the handles, circling his body as he does so. After he has circled once he must support himself on both hands, with his body above the horse, before circling once again, facing the opposite direction.

## Double Circles of Both Legs Facing Outwards

This is one of the most strenuous and technically difficult movements of all. The gymnast must circle his shoulders, hips and feet continuously and at the same time lift his legs over the handles at his rear and drop them down sharply at his front, keeping them straight all the time.

# New Movement
## The Flourish or Windmill

This movement forces the gymnast to clear his legs, moving each leg singly as in shears, and at the same time circle his body as he does in a double leg circle. He also executes a front vault round one handle, clearing his legs at the same time in an apparently wild—but in reality carefully controlled —fashion so as to keep his rhythm and balance.

# Still Rings

Recognized by all gymnasts as the hardest physically of all the apparatus, the rings provide a real test of even the strongest competitor's skill and strength. Indeed the names of some of the techniques—the 'Cross', the 'German Shoot' are just two—suggest a gladiatorial arena rather than a modern gymnasium!

It is important to remember that the rings must remain still throughout the gymnast's performance. As a result the gymnast has to put his body through some extraordinary distortions as he completes the movements. Shown first are some of the basic movements, such as the upstart and the uprise, that he uses to bring himself from, say, below the rings to a position above them. Competitors must also display strength, include movements of especial difficulty and finish with a dismount as technically difficult as the rest of the routine. Also shown are some of the hold positions and some of the new movements recently introduced.

## Basic Movements
### The Dislocation

The term dislocation sounds painful; all it means is turning the shoulder joint well within the capabilities of that part of the physique. The gymnast hangs upside down (the inverted hang) from the rings with his legs between the rings at right angles to his body. He then extends his hips and shoulder downwards and forwards.

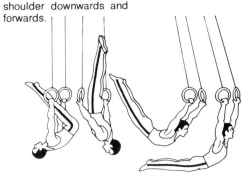

### The Upstart

'This move brings the gymnast's body up from below the apparatus. Because it is done without swinging forwards, it requires great strength. Starting in the inverted hang, the gymnast first straightens his hips and then, keeping his arms straight, raises his body so that he is sitting between the rings, in the 'L' or half lever position.

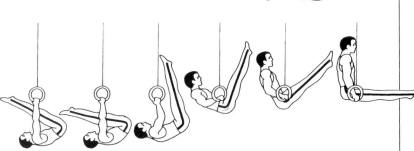

### The Uprise Forwards

Hanging under the rings, the gymnast must swing forwards and bring his body into the piked position. Immediately straightening his body, he raises it forwards and up into a sitting position (the 'L' or half lever), keeping his legs straight.

# Strength Movements
## From Handstand, Circle to Handstand

From a handstand the gymnast moves his shoulders forwards and his legs slowly down so that he is supporting himself between the rings. He continues turning backwards, bringing his feet forwards. Bending his arms slightly, he pulls at the rings, so moving his body upwards until he is able to thrust himself up into a handstand.

## Straight Body Lift to Handstand

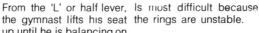

From the 'L' or half lever, the gymnast lowers his legs until his whole body is vertical and then leans forwards, grasping the rings with arms bent. He then 'see-saws' from his hands, bending and straightening his arms, finally raising himself into a handstand. The slightest amount of swing will lose a gymnast points.

From the 'L' or half lever, the gymnast lifts his seat up until he is balancing on his hands in the piked position. His shoulders must be far enough forwards to enable him to raise his legs into a handstand. This is most difficult because the rings are unstable.

## Press to Handstand or Elephant Lift

# Hold Positions
## Cross

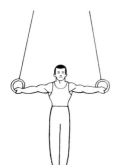

This position is maintained by tension resulting from the extension of the gymnast's body, rather than its contraction, as in some positions. The gymnast's shoulders must be in line with his hands. His body and legs must be absolutely straight, and he must not arch his back.

## Top Planche

This is dependent on muscular extension. The gymnast lies between the rings (*planche* is French for board, so as flat as a plank is an apt description!), keeping his body exactly horizontal and without arching his back. His shoulders must be far enough forward so that his body's centre of gravity is over his hands.

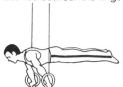

## Bottom Planche

In this position, the gymnast hangs below the rings, keeping his shoulders forwards and without arching his back.

# Movements of Maximum Difficulty

## Slow Circle through Cross

The gymnast circles anti-clockwise until he is hanging vertically. He then brings his body forwards, keeping his legs straight. He then lowers his legs and stretches his arms sideways so that he first lies horizontal and then hangs in a cross position. He completes the movement by moving into the 'L' or half lever.

## Uprise Forwards to Cross

The gymnast swings forwards and up so that he is lying between the rings with arms outstretched so that he forms a crucifix, arms extended and straight. This movement demands a highly developed sense of balance as well as considerable strength.

## Back Uprise to Handstand with Straight Arms

Starting in the inverted hang, the gymnast swings back, down and up between the rings. Then, thrusting with his arms, he moves up to a handstand. This movement was first performed by Menichelli of Italy.

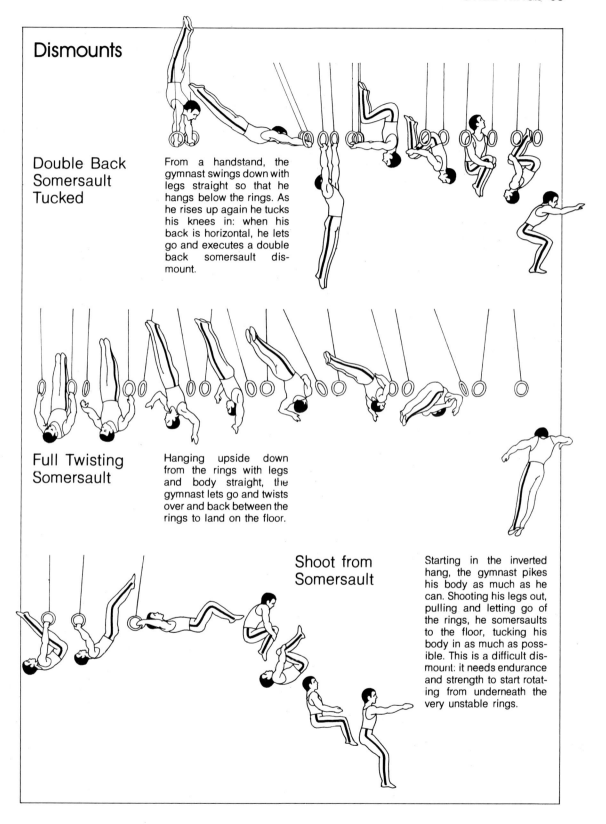

# Dismounts

## Double Back Somersault Tucked

From a handstand, the gymnast swings down with legs straight so that he hangs below the rings. As he rises up again he tucks his knees in: when his back is horizontal, he lets go and executes a double back somersault dismount.

## Full Twisting Somersault

Hanging upside down from the rings with legs and body straight, the gymnast lets go and twists over and back between the rings to land on the floor.

## Shoot from Somersault

Starting in the inverted hang, the gymnast pikes his body as much as he can. Shooting his legs out, pulling and letting go of the rings, he somersaults to the floor, tucking his body in as much as possible. This is a difficult dismount: it needs endurance and strength to start rotating from underneath the very unstable rings.

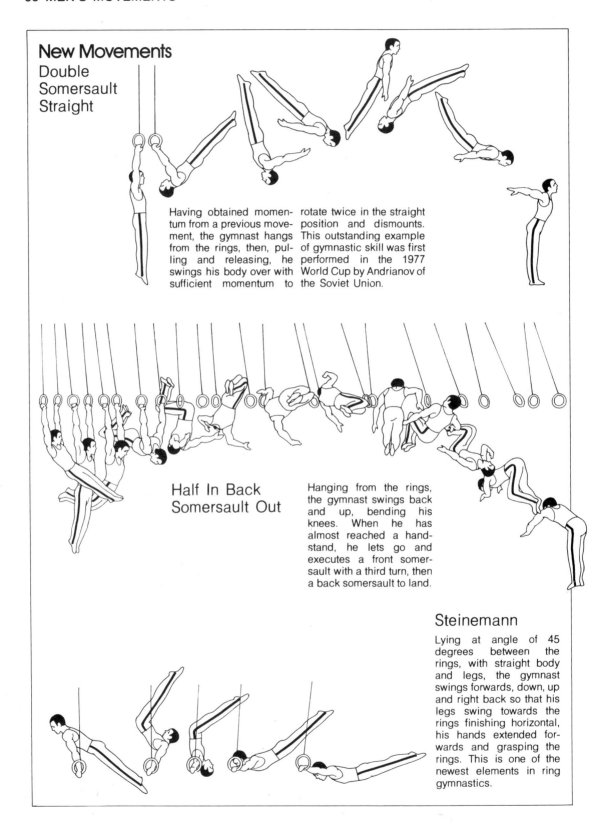

# New Movements
## Double Somersault Straight

Having obtained momentum from a previous movement, the gymnast hangs from the rings, then, pulling and releasing, he swings his body over with sufficient momentum to rotate twice in the straight position and dismounts. This outstanding example of gymnastic skill was first performed in the 1977 World Cup by Andrianov of the Soviet Union.

## Half In Back Somersault Out

Hanging from the rings, the gymnast swings back and up, bending his knees. When he has almost reached a handstand, he lets go and executes a front somersault with a third turn, then a back somersault to land.

## Steinemann

Lying at angle of 45 degrees between the rings, with straight body and legs, the gymnast swings forwards, down, up and right back so that his legs swing towards the rings finishing horizontal, his hands extended forwards and grasping the rings. This is one of the newest elements in ring gymnastics.

# Parallel Bars

Parallel bars are ideal for both beginners and more advanced performers; a wide variety of movements can be attempted, with the bars set higher or lower to suit the individual concerned. Though once enormous shoulder strength, endurance and sheer force might have meant success, today's performer must bring what amounts to an understanding of the mechanics of the body as well as balance, strength and style to his work on the bars.

In competition, gymnasts are required to execute moves that demonstrate both their strength and balancing ability. They must include what is known as an element of maximum difficulty; in this type of movement, the gymnast must release both his hands from the bars at the same moment and grip them again simultaneously. Advanced competitors will of course demonstrate their prowess by selecting particularly difficult starts and dismounts and may also incorporate one of the new movements developed in recent years. Some especially dramatic movements demanding all the gymnast's skills are also shown.

## Balances and Strength Movements

### Press to Handstand

This movement is usually done from the 'L' or half lever (a sitting position with legs at right angles to the body). Keeping his arms straight, the gymnast lifts his seat high to a piked balance (in which the body is folded into the thighs). Then, still keeping his arms straight, he raises himself to a handstand.

### Straight Body Press

From the sitting position, the gymnast lowers his legs and then raises them behind him, bending his arms to give momentum and keeping his body stiff. As his legs approach vertical, the gymnast must straighten his arms so that he completes the movement in a handstand.

### One-Hand Balance

This movement usually starts from the handstand. The gymnast swings his body over arm to one side, keeping his legs wide apart and stretching one arm out. In effect, he balances in the air on one hand, which supports his entire bodyweight.

# Movements of Maximum Difficulty

## Under Somersault to Handstand

This movement is every bit as difficult to do as it looks! From the support position (in which the body and legs are held horizontally above the bars) the gymnast swings his legs and body down through the bars. As his legs are about to turn again he extends them and somersaults upwards through the bars to a handstand.

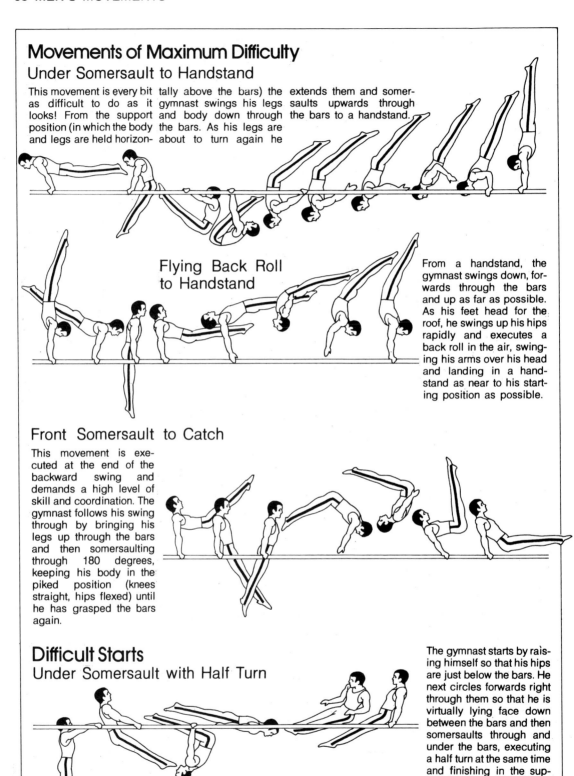

## Flying Back Roll to Handstand

From a handstand, the gymnast swings down, forwards through the bars and up as far as possible. As his feet head for the roof, he swings up his hips rapidly and executes a back roll in the air, swinging his arms over his head and landing in a handstand as near to his starting position as possible.

## Front Somersault to Catch

This movement is executed at the end of the backward swing and demands a high level of skill and coordination. The gymnast follows his swing through by bringing his legs up through the bars and then somersaulting through 180 degrees, keeping his body in the piked position (knees straight, hips flexed) until he has grasped the bars again.

# Difficult Starts
## Under Somersault with Half Turn

The gymnast starts by raising himself so that his hips are just below the bars. He next circles forwards right through them so that he is virtually lying face down between the bars and then somersaults through and under the bars, executing a half turn at the same time and finishing in the support position.

## Upstart Forwards Straddle Backwards

After circling forwards down and through the bars, the gymnast must somersault under, through and over the bars with sufficient force to be able to straddle them as he descends again. He finishes the movement by supporting himself with arms bent.

## Upstart Forwards 'Kips' Backwards

An upstart takes a gymnast from below to above the bars. He first pulls his legs inwards to a deep pike and then straightens them out again to achieve upward movement. Releasing his hands and placing them between his legs as he straddles the bars, then swings himself back and up so that he is parallel with the bars.

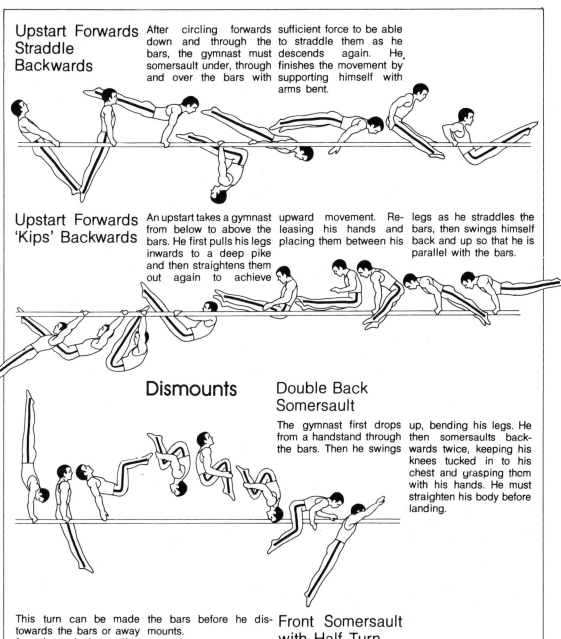

# Dismounts

## Double Back Somersault

The gymnast first drops from a handstand through the bars. Then he swings up, bending his legs. He then somersaults backwards twice, keeping his knees tucked in to his chest and grasping them with his hands. He must straighten his body before landing.

This turn can be made towards the bars or away from them—both are allotted the same level of difficulty. Starting in piked position, the gymnast swings down through the bars and up before executing a front somersault, at the same time half-turning so that he faces the other way. His legs and body must be horizontally above the bars before he dismounts.

## Front Somersault with Half Turn

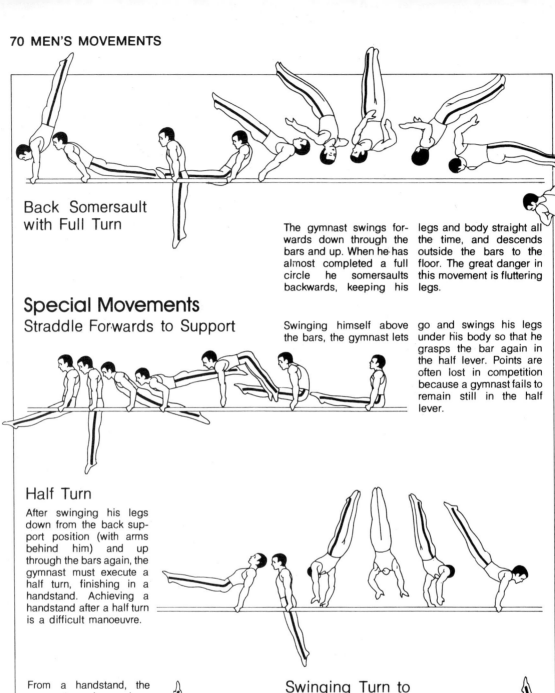

## Back Somersault with Full Turn

The gymnast swings forwards down through the bars and up. When he has almost completed a full circle he somersaults backwards, keeping his legs and body straight all the time, and descends outside the bars to the floor. The great danger in this movement is fluttering legs.

## Special Movements
### Straddle Forwards to Support

Swinging himself above the bars, the gymnast lets go and swings his legs under his body so that he grasps the bar again in the half lever. Points are often lost in competition because a gymnast fails to remain still in the half lever.

### Half Turn

After swinging his legs down from the back support position (with arms behind him) and up through the bars again, the gymnast must execute a half turn, finishing in a handstand. Achieving a handstand after a half turn is a difficult manoeuvre.

From a handstand, the gymnast swings down through the bars to the back support position and then must turn on one arm back to a handstand. This movement is the real test of a master gymnast: his legs must remain tight and he must take all the help he can from the swing in the bars.

### Swinging Turn to Handstand

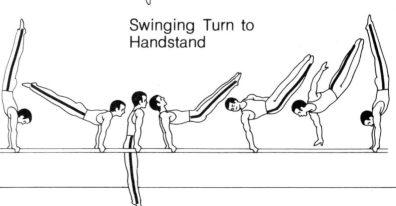

# New Movements

## The Flip-Kip

This movement is a complete circle. The gymnast first swings head down through the bars and up again so that his shins nearly touch his nose. Then he straightens the legs as he rises up and returns to the support position. It is very difficult to maintain contact with the bars while changing the hand position.

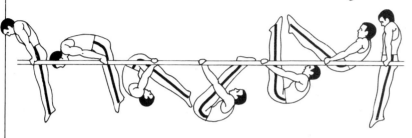

## Diamidov Turn

This is a full 180-degree turn from handstand to handstand. The gymnast supports himself on his left arm as he turns. The movement is named after the powerful Russian gymnast Sergei Diamidov, by whom it was first performed.

## Somersault from Upper Arms to Support

The gymnast swings his legs and body down, under and back through the bars. This gives him sufficient impetus to somer- sault forwards just after he reaches the horizontal position. He finishes in straight arm support. A movement that separates the men from the super- men, it was invented by Honma, a Japanese gymnast.

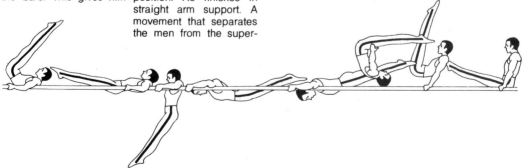

# Horizontal Bar

'Graceful', 'exciting'—all the claims made for a top gymnast's performance on the horizontal bar must surely be justified.

Use of the body's suppleness and strength, correct hand grips and elegance and style—not mere force—all bring a gymnast success on the horizontal bar. Beginners commonly fail to let their momentum and technique create the movement: force only interferes with rhythm and swing.

Essentially, work on the horizontal bar consists of swinging round it in both close and long circles, without stopping, using a variety of grasps and maintaining a central position on the bar. Movements of especial interest are the upstart or kip, in which the performer swings himself over the bar, and those movements which require him to release the bar with both hands and grasp it again. A number of dismounts are available to complete the routine. Also shown are a number of movements named after the gymnasts who first developed them.

The main grasps on the horizontal bar are *undergrasp, overgrasp* and *cross grasp* (one hand undergrasp, one hand overgrasp). Whatever the grasp, the gymnast must always be rotating his grasp around the bar with his thumbs leading. Thus the gymnast swinging around the bar with the back of the body leading the way, would use the undergrasp, and swinging around the bar with his chest leading, would use the overgrasp. Swinging in the wrong direction with the wrong grasp merely peels the gymnast from the bar. If this 'rule of thumb' is applied, the gymnast may cross his hands or reverse his hands without fear of falling.

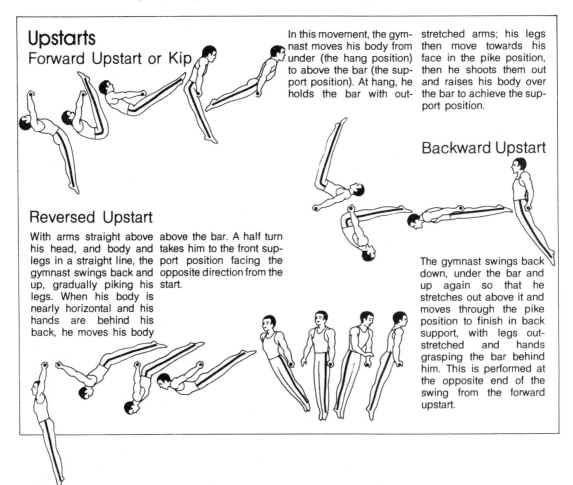

## Upstarts
### Forward Upstart or Kip

In this movement, the gymnast moves his body from under (the hang position) to above the bar (the support position). At hang, he holds the bar with outstretched arms; his legs then move towards his face in the pike position, then he shoots them out and raises his body over the bar to achieve the support position.

### Reversed Upstart

With arms straight above his head, and body and legs in a straight line, the gymnast swings back and up, gradually piking his legs. When his body is nearly horizontal and his hands are behind his back, he moves his body above the bar. A half turn takes him to the front support position facing the opposite direction from the start.

### Backward Upstart

The gymnast swings back down, under the bar and up again so that he stretches out above it and moves through the pike position to finish in back support, with legs outstretched and hands grasping the bar behind him. This is performed at the opposite end of the swing from the forward upstart.

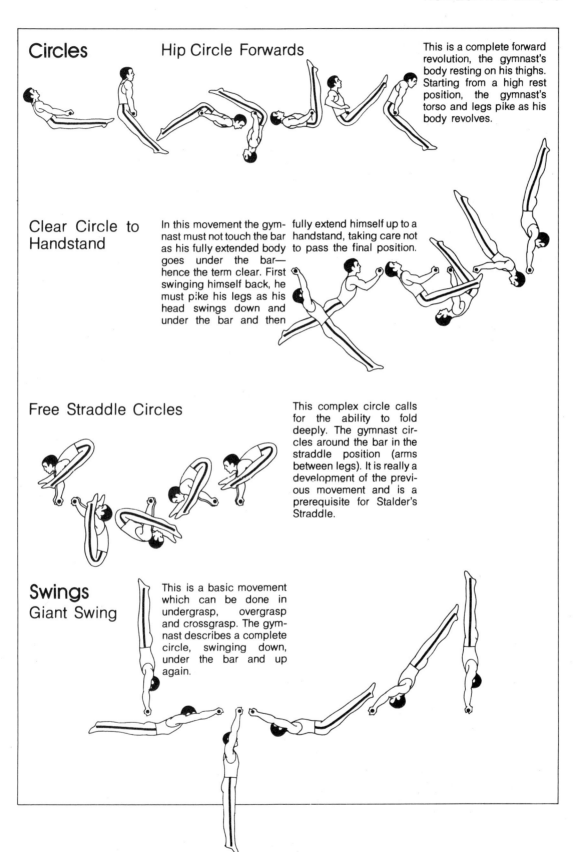

# Circles

## Hip Circle Forwards

This is a complete forward revolution, the gymnast's body resting on his thighs. Starting from a high rest position, the gymnast's torso and legs pike as his body revolves.

## Clear Circle to Handstand

In this movement the gymnast must not touch the bar as his fully extended body goes under the bar—hence the term clear. First swinging himself back, he must pike his legs as his head swings down and under the bar and then fully extend himself up to a handstand, taking care not to pass the final position.

## Free Straddle Circles

This complex circle calls for the ability to fold deeply. The gymnast circles around the bar in the straddle position (arms between legs). It is really a development of the previous movement and is a prerequisite for Stalder's Straddle.

# Swings
## Giant Swing

This is a basic movement which can be done in undergrasp, overgrasp and crossgrasp. The gymnast describes a complete circle, swinging down, under the bar and up again.

## Back Hang Swing or Steinemann Swing

Starting in the back support position, the gymnast travels backwards up, over the bar in a piked position, right round, up again, over—and on and on *ad infinitum*, in a manner all too reminiscent of a medieval torture chamber.

## Eagle Swing

Swinging first forwards with his body fully extended (the layout), then backwards, the gymnast passes under the bar, rises up into a pike and then straightens up as he reaches the handstand.

# Movements Releasing and Regrasping the Bar

## Vault to Catch

Rising backwards, the gymnast swings over the top of the bar. As he does so, he turns, catching the bar on the other side as he descends. This move was developed from the traditional rear vault on the Box.

## Somersault to Catch

Starting with a backward swing under the bar and up again, the gymnast then somersaults above it. As he descends, with legs apart he must catch hold of the bar at the same spot at which he left it.

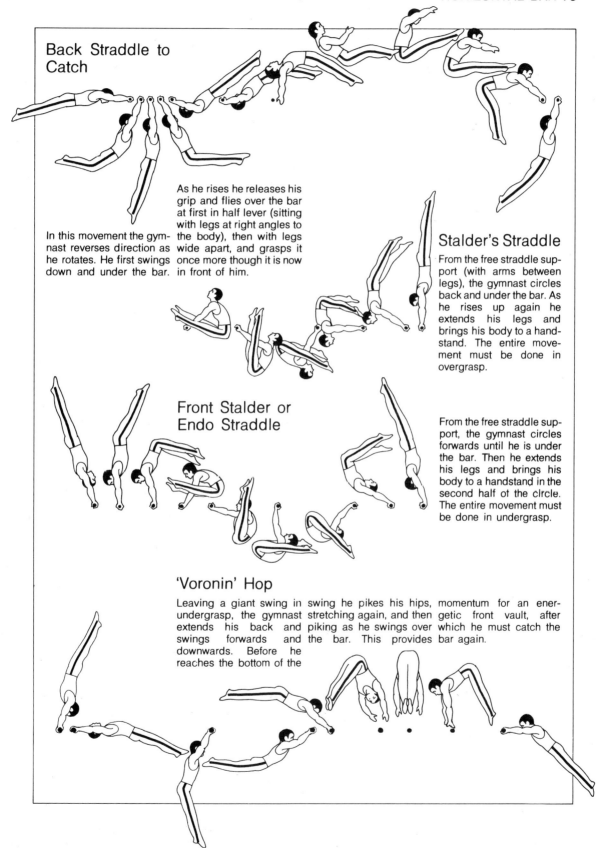

## Back Straddle to Catch

In this movement the gymnast reverses direction as he rotates. He first swings down and under the bar.

As he rises he releases his grip and flies over the bar at first in half lever (sitting with legs at right angles to the body), then with legs wide apart, and grasps it once more though it is now in front of him.

## Stalder's Straddle

From the free straddle support (with arms between legs), the gymnast circles back and under the bar. As he rises up again he extends his legs and brings his body to a handstand. The entire movement must be done in overgrasp.

## Front Stalder or Endo Straddle

From the free straddle support, the gymnast circles forwards until he is under the bar. Then he extends his legs and brings his body to a handstand in the second half of the circle. The entire movement must be done in undergrasp.

## 'Voronin' Hop

Leaving a giant swing in undergrasp, the gymnast extends his back and swings forwards and downwards. Before he reaches the bottom of the swing he pikes his hips, stretching again, and then piking as he swings over the bar. This provides momentum for an energetic front vault, after which he must catch the bar again.

# Dismounts
## Long Fly

This movement must be performed with legs together and straight. The gymnast swings down and under the bar, raises himself over it, swings his legs upwards, kicking them downwards to dismount.

## Front Away with Half Turn

The gymnast swings over the bar, down under and up. As he reaches a horizontal position again, he lets go of the bar, half twists in the air and descends to the ground.

## Triple-back Somersault

The gymnast swings down and under the bar. When he reaches horizontal again, he lets go, somersaults backwards three times and lands—gracefully perhaps—on the floor.

# Modern Rhythmic Gymnastics

Modern Rhythmic Gymnastics is a rapidly developing branch of gymnastics. It came to prominence early this century in Germany as a variation of classical ballet and was developed by the Eastern European countries as a competitive sport with a strong leaning towards balletic techniques.

The first World Championships were held in Budapest in 1962 when the F.I.G. gave recognition to the sport. Although these Championships are held every two years, Modern Rhythmic Gymnastics has not been accepted into the Olympics and it seems unlikely that it will appear at Moscow in 1980.

The sport is performed by women and consists solely of floor exercises, performed both without apparatus, and with small hand apparatus—ball, hoop, rope, ribbon, and clubs.

The basic exercises without apparatus demand suppleness, coordination, control, spring, vitality, gracefulness, elegance, and feeling. Body movements—jumps, leaps, turns, steps, balances, waves, and bends —are performed as a smooth, flowing, linked sequence, choreographed to a musical accompaniment. Apparatus must be seen to be part of the gymnast and her performance.

*The ball* is plastic or rubber, slightly smaller than a normal size football, and is especially weighted (minimum of 400 grammes ($14\frac{1}{4}$ ounces)) for easy handling. It has a smooth surface, and can be any colour.

*The hoop* may be plastic, fibreglass, or wooden, and sizes can vary to suit the gymnast, but for senior international competition the hoop must be the regulation diameter of between 80 and 90 centimetres (2 feet $7\frac{1}{2}$ inches and 2 feet $11\frac{1}{2}$ inches).

*The rope* has no handles, and is simply of a length proportionate to the height of the gymnast.

*The ribbon* is made of satin material, 6 metres (20 feet) long, and 4 to 6 centimetres ($1\frac{1}{2}$ to $2\frac{1}{2}$ inches) wide. It is attached to a wooden, plastic, or fibreglass stick, between 50 and 60 centimetres (1 foot $2\frac{1}{2}$ inches and 1 foot $11\frac{3}{4}$ inches) in length. It usually has a swivel attachment, allowing a completely free movement of the ribbon around the stick.

*The clubs* are perhaps the most complex of all the apparatus, partly because the gymnast usually works with two at once. They are made of wood or plastic, and are of a minimum weight of 150 grammes (5 ounces) each.

Each piece of apparatus has certain obvious characteristics of its own—the ball for bouncing and rolling; the hoop for rotation, rolling, and stepping through; the rope for skipping; the clubs for swinging and circling; and the ribbon for making graceful, flowing patterns. Each piece is thrown in different ways and to different heights, and the techniques of throwing and catching are an important part of the exercise. Equally important is work with the free hand.

Movements to look for are spin turns, jumps, and back bends, which are performed while the apparatus is being kept constantly in motion, and incorporated with these body movements. Marks are awarded in competition for certain difficult elements, and for the choreography, use of the 12 metre (13 yard) square floor space, the originality of the exercise, technical performance, and harmony between movement and music.

Modern Rhythmic Gymnastics is performed by both individuals and groups. One gymnast is expected to perform solo and in a group. In competition, a group sequence is composed for six gymnasts, working with six pieces of apparatus. Team members work in unison, showing intricate floor patterns and exchanges of apparatus.

Whether performed as a solo or a group item, in a competitive aspect or purely as demonstration, Modern Rhythmic Gymnastics is very aesthetic, and appealing to the spectator. It is very graceful and flowing, and the intricate skills with the apparatus, linked with extended and full body movements, at times leave the spectator quite speechless.

Erica Schiller of the Soviet Union performing with the
ball. The associations of Modern Rhythmic Gymnastics
with ballet are evident in this picture.

# Sports Acrobatics

Sports Acrobatics is another branch of gymnastics which has not yet achieved Olympic status. It has been established as an international sport since the World Acrobatics Championships in Moscow in June 1974, held under the auspices of the newly-formed International Federation of Sports Acrobatics (I.F.S.A.).

'Whilst we in western Europe were developing an approach to acrobatics, Asia and European Russia were developing a system.' This remark of John Atkinson, British National Gymnastics Coach and I.F.S.A. Executive Committee member, underlines the superiority of Russia and China based on an age-old tradition of acrobatics in these countries. Many of the acrobats of stage and circus emerged from the Russian or Chinese circus schools, and not a few found their way into entertainment acrobatics from a successful background in the sport there.

The hallmark of 'Sports Acro' as against other forms of acrobatics is that no apparatus is involved.

Vladimir Machuga and Vassily Pochivalov of the Soviet Union perform a hold-out on knees in the horizontal position in the men's pairs. The Russians hold most of the titles in Sports Acrobatics.

In meets under I.F.S.A. rules there are major competitions in seven events: women's acrobatic jumps, men's acrobatic jumps, men's pairs, mixed pairs, women's pairs, women's trios and men's group exercises (with four men).

The jumps are executed with a straight run up at even or accelerating speed, usually ending in a series of somersaults. There are penalties here for repetition of the same somersault elements.

The pairs and group exercises consist of a variety of supports, handstands, balances and pyramids (for all of which minimum hold times are laid down) and final exercises done to music.

Most of the competition is on a carpeted floor 12 metres (13 yards) square. Acrobatic jumping is performed on a special track 25 metres (27 yards) long, 1.5 metres (5 feet) wide and 30 centimetres (one foot) thick.

There are two compulsory and two voluntary exercises in the preliminary rounds and two voluntary exercises alone in the finals. Much as in artistic gymnastics, the final ranking in each event is based on the average of the highest compulsory and voluntary scores in the preliminaries added to the two voluntary scores in the final.

There are six judges—the superior and five others. The superior judge assesses difficulty rating and times the hold positions in handstands and pyramids and the final exercises. The other judges evaluate the execution of the exercise by reference to a list of faults laid down by the I.F.S.A. The declared mark is the average of the superior judge's mark and the middle mark of the five others.

The last decade has seen tremendous improvements in Sports Acrobatics work. It is now not uncommon to see triple back somersaults on the floor, and the quadruple back somersault cannot be far away, given the inexhaustible wealth of creative imagination which seems to be the stock in trade of the Soviet and Chinese acrobatics coaches.

Irina Zagorny and Vadim Pissmeniy of the Soviet Union in the mixed pairs. Mixed pairs are for many people the highlight of Sports Acrobatics. It is the only time in gymnastics that male and female compete together for a single score as a result of their combined skills.

# Gymnastics
# Around the World

# Europe

## Josef Göhler

One of Europe's first gymnastic artists was the Italian Archange Tuccaro, who learned the art of the floor exercise at the court of the Kings of France and then developed it. In 1599, he wrote a manual of floor exercises (and horse vaulting) from which it appears that he had already mastered the aerial somersault and the long fly.

International gymnastics for men goes back to 1896, when gymnasts from Germany (from Berlin to be exact) and several other countries took part in the Olympic Games, with apparatus work as a permanent feature. But the equipment was very primitive as neither the parallel bars nor the horizontal bar were pre-stressed and the round pommels and the long heavy body of the horse prevented a broader approach to gymnastics.

After World War II, the Finns won the 1948 Olympic Games in London with their team victory over the favourites, the Swiss, who still trained in the old style of two to three hours three times a week. The Finns, under Dr Birger Stenman, trained daily for weeks, if not months. But their dream of victory was short-lived for at Helsinki in 1952 they gave way to the Russians and the Swiss and were lucky not to be beaten by the Japanese, who did surprisingly well with only five gymnasts.

The Russians and Japanese then started a long duel at World Championships and Olympic Games, until the Japanese gained superiority and held it from 1960 to 1976. And now which European nations can keep pace with the two giants?

The East German male gymnasts captured third place in the World Championships in 1974 and second place in the European Championships in 1977. They have Brückner, Bärthel, the excellent horse and horizontal bar gymnast Nikolay, Mack and Jensch: no country can offer as many quality gymnasts, not even West Germany with its top trio Gienger, Thuene and Rohrwick; nor Hungary, with the Donath, Molnar, Magyar and Kovacs quartet; nor Rumania with an equivalent team, and certainly not Poland which now has only Szajna as a gymnast in the world class. Switzerland has Bretscher, and France has Boerio, but neither country has enough talented gymnasts to make up marks in the lower categories.

Gymnastics in Europe has profited greatly from technical achievements. The German Richard Reuther designed the sprung springboard. The chemical industry produced foam rubber for soft mats and the Schnitzel foam rubber trench for double and triple somersaults that were too dangerous in the past. The new pommelled horse with its narrower, shorter body and the wider pommels has permitted exercises that could not

*Opposite:* Eberhard Gienger, probably the best gymnast ever produced by West Germany, doing the German Giant.

be dreamt of ten years ago. The Hungarian Zoltan Magyar has become a pioneer of gymnastics in the Cross position, first demonstrated in Europe by the American Kurt Thomas in 1976. The 'flying scissors', a daring spread-leg movement of an entirely new kind, was quickly taken up by Europe's best and is now mastered with almost as much virtuosity as by America's 'gymnast of the year', Kurt Thomas, and the specialists Ulloah and Marcy.

Since 1955, there have been European Championships and almost every country has a major international meeting and several other international events in its annual programme. Day and residential training centres are to be found not only in the Eastern Bloc: the West Germans, too, and the Swiss, Italians and French are trying to improve their young talent in this way. The Eastern Bloc countries have the advantage, however, that in their social system sports enjoy greater prestige and, consequently, problems of schooling and vocation do not press as strongly as in the countries of the West.

Hungarian Eva Ovari performing a movement on the beam which requires positive range of movement and real muscular strength, as indicated by the contraction in her left thigh.

It is therefore hardly surprising that the Eastern Bloc countries dominate international gymnastics. Taking the best performances of the five top performers in the 1977 European Championships we obtain the following order of merit: the Soviet Union, East Germany, West Germany, Hungary, Rumania, Switzerland, Czechoslovakia, Bulgaria, Italy, France. Only Poland has dropped out, since the Kubica brothers gave up gymnastics. Gienger was only a short way behind the top Russians in the free exercise event in the 1977 European Championships, yet he can hardly be ranked much above the East Germans Brückner, Bärthel and Nikolay, or Thuene, who fled to West Germany from the East in 1975 and will qualify for the German Gymnastics Federation team this year.

In women's gymnastics Hungary, East Germany and, since 1972, Rumania rank top among the European nations. Vera Caslavska of Czechoslovakia was the first European gymnast to draw huge crowds. Then Ludmilla Tourischeva of the Soviet Union reigned supreme until she was dethroned by a 14-year-old girl, Nadia Comaneci

*Opposite:* Eberhard Gienger, the strong man of the West German team and one of the contenders for the World and Olympic honours, on the parallel bars performing a front somersault to catch. He is at present World Champion on the horizontal bars.

*Above:* This cartwheel on the beam, executed by Steffi Kraeker of East Germany, demonstrates the depth of technical excellence long associated with her country's training system.

*Below:* Van Elteren, former junior and senior champion of Holland, performing the bottom planche. This popular young gymnast is one of several exceptionally elegant Dutch gymnasts.

from Rumania, who was trained by Bela Karoly. Karoly adopted a training programme aimed at mastering the international repertoire by the age of 12 if possible. Similar training is available to 10- and 11-year-olds in Czechoslovakia and to 12- and 13-year-olds in East Germany and Hungary.

The order of merit of women's teams according to the best performances in the 1977 World Championships is as follows: the Soviet Union, Rumania, East Germany, Hungary, Czechoslovakia, West Germany, Bulgaria, Italy, France, Poland, Great Britain, the Netherlands and Norway.

The Rumanians Nadia Comaneci and Teodora Ungureanu must be regarded as the recent best performers, though it appears that they may lose something of their shine if the 14- and 15-year-old 'wonder children' from the Soviet Union continue to advance. The East Germans Kraeker, Hindorff, Grabolle, Trantow and Kunhardt, the Hungarians Egervari and Csanyi, the Czechs Mareckova, Cerna and Holkovickova or the West German Andrea Bieger will only be able to rival the Soviet girls by performing their free exercises without a fault.

Many, indeed most, of the twenty top women gymnasts of Europe are less than 15 years old, an astonishing but also sobering phenomenon which, due to the heavy risk in this high performance sport, gives educationalists, psychologists and physiologists something to think about and trainers a great deal of worry.

*Opposite:* The most famous name in American gymnastics, Cathy Rigby is a commentator for ABC. She was World Medallist on the beam in 1970. She is seen here half way through a turn.

Zoltan Magyar of Hungary doing the back shears under the scrutiny of judges and television camera. Magyar has received a 10 for his work on the pommelled horse.

# The United States

## Muriel Grossfeld

The U.S.G.F. (United States Gymnastics Federation) is the governing body of gymnastics in the United States and the many organizations that run gymnastics programmes are members of it. Programmes run by the N.C.A.A. (National Collegiate Athletic Association), the N.A.I.A. (National Association of Intercollegiate Athletics), and the A.I.W.A. (Association for Intercollegiate Women's Athletics) have grown very large. The A.A.U. (Amateur Athletics Union), the former governing body of gymnastics programmes, has become very small, but still has national championships for junior and elite competitors. Many other organizations, such as the Y.M.C.A., Sokols, Turners, Recreational and Park Departments and Jewish Centres, run programmes of varying sizes.

The U.S.G.F. runs local and national age group competitions at beginners', intermediate and advanced levels for boys and girls from 9 years old upwards. For elite or future international competitors the U.S.G.F. has a junior national team programme and a national team programme for boys and girls. The members of the team are the top ten (for women) and the top twenty (for men) all

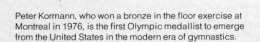

Peter Kormann, who won a bronze in the floor exercise at Montreal in 1976, is the first Olympic medallist to emerge from the United States in the modern era of gymnastics.

*Right:* Linda Kardos, interesting, exciting and original in performance, typifies the style of gymnastics produced in the United States. She is seen here at the 1977 Coca Cola International.

Kurt Thomas, acclaimed as one of the most consistent all around American gymnasts and one of the best prospects for future Olympic medals, performing the Cross at the 1977 N.C.A.A.

been a positive force in the development of American and world gymnastics. Innovations like the wood-covered fibreglass poles for the uneven parallel (asymmetric) bars are helping the technical growth of the sport as well as increasing the safety of the gymnasts.

The regulations and procedures are constantly being examined by the U.S.G.F. committees and are modified or changed at times, contributing to the safety and longevity of the gymnasts and still allowing performances to meet all other F.I.G. standards.

The open scoring system is being used again in some U.S.G.F. competitions. The U.S.G.F. is in favour of this because it produces a more open and healthier general climate.

Television has been more responsible for the popularity of gymnastics in the United States than anything other than the work of the U.S.G.F. and dedicated gymnastics pioneers. All three major networks, Public Television, and local stations televise gymnastics events quite regularly.

For many years United States gymnastics could support only one publication, the *International Gymnast*, often at the extreme personal financial sacrifice of its publisher, Glenn Sundby. At the present time, several national magazines and newsletters are surviving as well as many regional and state publications.

The increasing number of international gymnastics exchanges has played an important part in the growth, rising quality and popularity of gymnastics in the United States. Tours of teams from other nations have produced revenue for gymnastics and at the same time brought the work of the world's finest gymnasts to the American people. The U.S.G.F. has tried to balance the events geographically, so that gymnasts, coaches and judges have had fine opportunities to learn from the best.

Another important aspect of these international events is the participation, either in exhibition or competition, of United States gymnasts and officials. These opportunities have greatly accelerated the growing maturity and confidence of athletes and officials, raised the level of gymnastics knowledge in the United States and caused the rest of the gymnastics world to become aware of young American gymnasts' talent and performance abilities.

The U.S.G.F. American Cup is a major international individual competition hosting the world's finest men and women gymnasts for optional all around competition. Its format is optional all around competition on the first day and all around finals on the second day. The last three American Cups (1976-8) have been held in Madison Square Garden in New York City, one of America's finest and most renowned arenas.

around competitors in the United States Championships which are held each spring. The junior national team (20 girls and 20 boys) is by selection. The strength of the girls' programme comes from small independent clubs or schools, a few of which have excellent facilities, coaches and elite programmes and develop most of America's top gymnasts.

Both the men and women have developed well organized and efficient national judges' associations for providing extensive education, seminar and testing programmes. They also assign the properly qualified officials for all sanctioned competitions and help all the organizations that run gymnastics competitions.

United States equipment manufacturers have

So far, national competitions held this year, leading up to the World Championships, indicate that the United States will be quite a bit stronger than in the Montreal Olympics. Donna Turnbow, 1977 National All Around Champion, was injured in the autumn, but reports indicate that she is back to full training and is looking very good. Kathy Johnson, 1977 American Cup Champion, was also injured, but only a fall from the balance beam, perhaps her best event, prevented her from winning again this year. Leslie Russo has had an exceptional year, improving her difficulty and performance in all four events. In the Joachim Blume Barcelona Invitational she won second place in the all around and first place on the bars. In the *Chunichi* Cup in Tokyo she won second place on floor and bars and first place on the beam. 1977 National Team members Lisa Cawthorn and Sharon Shapiro are also looking good. A new gymnast to the national scene is 14-year-old 1977 uneven parallel (asymmetric) bars phenomenon, Marcia Frederick. She was placed second in the all around to Russo in the first national elite meet of this season, proving her all around ability. Her work on the bars is superior to anything United States coaches and judges have seen in world competition. She somersaults and twists with ease, but is an absolute master of swing which she shows off in her Stalder shoots and toe circles to handstands.

It looks as if several gymnasts from the new junior national team programme will be very strong competitors for the 1978 World Championships team. Merilyn Chapman surprised the gymnastics world when she won the all around in the first British World Invitational over an international field that included Soviet National Team member Olga Koval. Kelly McCoy is improving her performance quality and stability. Leslie Phifer has some good solid difficulty (double back and double twist on the floor). The most improved member of the team is 12-year-old Jackie Cassello. Jackie will be too young for the 1978 team, but look out for her very difficult and charismatic performances and great vaulting by 1980. Rhonda Schwann is impressing all the experts with her terrific work on the bars and her tumbling and vaulting skills. Gigi Ambandos and Linda Kardos do not have as much difficulty, but are turning in consistently strong all around performances.

Experts feel that Kurt Thomas is the finest male gymnast ever produced in the United States. His basic techniques and swings are almost impeccable as displayed in his domination of the 1978 American Cup. Bart Connor is still improving and looks like a sure World Championships team member. Mike Wilson is surprising everyone with his improvements and ability to turn in high totals in the all around. Peter Kormann, bronze medallist

Donna Turnbow, 1977 National All Around Champion and winner of the 1978 'Champions All' in London, where her consistency and technical depth were brought to the fore.

in floor exercises in Montreal, will be in top form for the World Championships. Gene Whelan also continues to impress, and most United States gymnastic experts feel the men's World Championships team will be very strong.

Seventeen-year-old phenomenon Jimmy Hartung looks as if he may become a member of the 1978 World Championships team. Phil Kahoy Jr. has been pushing Jimmy in their competitions and shows promise of becoming a fine national competitor. Peter Stout is strong in every event and shows promising virtuosity on the pommelled horse. Look out for 12-year-old Chris Riegel and his exceptional all around ability.

Certainly the outstanding name in United States gymnastics continues to be Frank Bare. His leadership, internationally as well as domestically, continues to be an asset to all who love the sport of gymnastics.

# The Soviet Union

## Yuri Titov

Soviet gymnastics made its debut on the world scene in the 1952 Helsinki Olympics. New elements such as circles on the pommelled horse and turns on the horizontal bar helped the Soviet Union to dominate the gymnastic events. Since that first appearance, Soviet gymnasts have won forty-six Olympic titles and gained thirty-eight World Championships, and every year gymnasts participate in over fifty international contests at home and abroad.

The Soviet Union soon gained the lead in women's gymnastics, when Larisa Latynina took the overall titles in the 1956 Melbourne Olympics and the 1964 Tokyo Olympics. Today Soviet gymnastics is world renowned through the careers of such famous stars as Nelli Kim, Natalia Tereshchenko, Maria Filatova, Olga Korbut, Ludmilla Tourischeva and Natalia Shaposhnikova.

Soviet success in international gymnastics is largely due to the scientific basis of the Soviet physical education system. Researchers at the Institute of Physical Culture's gymnastics department work out training methods for various ages and study ways of improving the teaching of gymnastic exercises.

But the most scientific methods are of little use unless ways are found to tap the potential of young people. The Soviet Gymnastics Federation is organized on a national, republic and city level. Its aim is to establish a specialized sports school for gymnastics in every town and district of the Soviet Union. The President of the Federation is involved in long-term planning at town and republic level and ensures that adequate provision is made for building new gymnastics facilities.

Children usually start serious gymnastics at the age of 7 or 8 by attending one of the 3000 gymnasia in the Soviet Union. The facilities and standards of equipment will vary according to how the gymnasia have been financed—some from municipal funds, some from trade union funds, some from district councils and others directly from central government. The classes are always taken by experienced or specially qualified coaches. Out of the 4500 specially trained coaches 3000 have attended college or university. The numbers are supplemented by trainers who have personal experience without formal training qualifications. Students studying to be gymnastics coaches train at special physical education colleges and receive a grant like all other students.

Aspiring gymnasts attend classes before or after school, or, if they are working, in the evenings. They go to a local gymnasium and are brought together in groups varying in size from 100 to 600 members. They are graded according to age and ability and are taken through the recommended exercise programmes. These classification programmes progress from simple to more compli-

*Opposite:* Olga Koval, one of the flock of high-class Soviet gymnasts, seems still a child but has all the quality one would expect to find in a more mature gymnast. She is shown here doing the aerial cartwheel phase of a dismount.

*Below:* The strength and suppleness of the back and shoulders are emphasized in this leap performed by another youthful Russian girl, Antonina Glebova.

*Bottom:* Alexandr Dityatin, overall champion of the Sixth U.S.S.R. People's Games of 1975 and bronze medallist in the 1975 European Championships, on the pommelled horse.

cated exercises. This is the only way a gymnast can tackle a new element. He must do the preparatory exercises and develop the strength of his muscles, the flexibility of his joints and his powers of coordination to the level demanded by the new element.

The young gymnast may then go in for the 'Master of Sports' classification programme which is instituted by the International Gymnastics Association and takes the gymnast to Olympic level.

Competition is considered to be an essential part of the training process, as important as regular training sessions. Competitions take place between parallel classes in sports schools, then between schools in one district, then between cities and so on, up the scale to the Soviet Championship where teams from all the fifteen Soviet republics compete with one another and with teams from Moscow and Leningrad.

Children who wish to attend sports schools do not have to pay fees since the coaches are paid by the state and the cost of equipment is borne either by a trade union or by the authorities. The cost of taking part in regional and national competitions, including fares and board and lodging, are also paid for.

*Opposite:* Nikolai Andrianov of the Soviet Union doing a Voronin Hop on the horizontal bar. Dynamic propulsion from the bar is an integral part of the movement.

Medical supervision of gymnasts is strict and people are allowed to go in for gymnastics only if they are in good health. Special physical culture clinics run by the Soviet Ministry of Health keep a check on practising gymnasts.

In recent years the trend has been towards younger and younger gymnasts making up the Soviet team. Maria Filatova won a gold medal in the Montreal Olympics in 1976 to celebrate her fifteenth birthday and Svetlana Agapova, who is only 14, is already in the world class on the uneven parallel (asymmetric) bars and in the floor exercise. She is already rated the ninth best woman gymnast in the world and her Korbut style of gymnastics will surely bring her many followers in future years. Another young, talented gymnast is Natalia Yurchenko, who is only 12 and is already being coached by top trainers.

In the men's team, Nikolai Andrianov is still the top Soviet male gymnast despite being five years older than the team's average. Andrianov won the 1976 Olympic overall title showing his great agility in the floor exercise and his strength on the rings. Twenty-year-old Vladimir Markelov is Andrianov's heir apparent. He was unbeaten throughout 1977, taking the individual title in the World Student Games and leading the Soviet Union to their first team victory over the Japanese for many years.

In the next Olympic Games, to be held in Moscow in 1980, Soviet gymnasts are looking forward to extending their hospitality to fellow gymnasts from all over the world.

Elena Mukhina, 1976 Soviet Union Youth Champion, shown here turning into an elegant backward walkover in the floor exercise.

European, World and Olympic Champion Nikolai Andrianov displaying his inimitable style in this execution of the rear vault on the pommelled horse.

# Great Britain

## Peter Aykroyd

Susan Cheesebrough has represented Great Britain in numerous international competitions, including the Montreal Olympics.

The British Amateur Gymnastics Association (B.A.G.A.), the controlling body of gymnastics in Britain, finds it difficult to supply exact figures on how the sport has mushroomed. But two sets of statistics are startling. Ten years ago, there were some 1500 gymnasts in Greater London. Today, there are over 8000, most of whom are girls. And since 1971, more than two million children have participated in the sport's basic training programme—the *Sunday Times*/B.A.G.A. Awards Scheme.

For many budding gymnasts, the Awards Scheme is their introduction to progressive training. But first, they must join a club. If they are lucky, they will be able to join their school gymnastics club which is likely to be affiliated to a regional schools' gymnastics association.

Gymnastics is not usually part of the school curriculum so school gym clubs have to operate out of school time. The schools' associations organize championships so a good gymnast can become a National Champion through the schools' network. Otherwise, young gymnasts must apply to join their local gymnastics club. In almost every case, the local club will have a lengthy waiting list and some names are put on waiting lists at birth. The patient gymnast is then rewarded with a test, and, if successful, becomes a member of the club. The boom in gymnastics has been responsible for full membership capacity in local clubs and in many cases the size of the clubs has been limited by the number of experienced coaches available.

The new member will join a section of the club to learn basic positions from a club coach. The club will be affiliated to the British Amateur Gymnastics Association through its region and this encourages coaches to become qualified through official coaching courses. Many coaches become judges and they, too, must be qualified before taking part in important events.

The young gymnast with promise may be asked to join an elite squad in the club to undergo extra training. It is at this stage that many gymnasts have to decide whether to do gymnastics just for fun or whether the long, hard training ahead is worthwhile. For a gymnast in a top club such as Ladywell, Tameside, Falcon Spartak or Swansea Y.M.C.A., the training, together with self-effort, can lead fairly quickly to national or even international honours. For the majority of gymnasts, though, the road to the top leads through championships organized by county and regional associations. Once a promising gymnast has been

*Opposite:* The Soviet Union's Nelli Kim, who was champion at the World Championships in 1974 and scored 10 for her vault in the Montreal Olympics, seen here doing an arabesque on the beam.

*Pages 96-7:* Ludmilla Tourischeva of the Soviet Union in a beautifully elegant movement on the beam—a delicately balanced side splits.

Eddie Arnold, number one in Britain in 1978 and the most consistent British gymnast.

Karen Leighton, medallist at the Maccebiah Games in Israel in 1977. Her performance at the Coca Cola international in 1977 established her as one of the leading British gymnasts.

picked out, the coaching becomes more personalized and the bond between coach and gymnast can last throughout the gymnast's competitive career.

A development in recent years has been the organization of a squad system which is designed to make sure that promising gymnasts receive expert coaching as early as possible. Squads are run at area and regional level and, of course, at national level. Standards throughout are maintained by national development plans conceived and produced through the Association.

As its name implies, the Association brings together many organizations which have an interest in gymnastics. It coordinates the activities of the sport not only within a national framework of directives but also according to policy laid down by the F.I.G.

Three national staff coaches are responsible for seeing that high standards of training are met within the regions all over the country. They hold coaching courses, guide clubs, pass on new techniques and look out for new talent. They also supervise the training—helped by assistant national coaches—of the national squads from whom members of British international teams are drawn. For the gymnast, the culmination of training is the various British championships which attract the best gymnasts in the country.

Under general training comes the *Sunday Times*/B.A.G.A. Awards Scheme. The Scheme is simple. It has four grades and children can be trained and tested by their teachers and coaches. Once a child has passed a grade, he or she can obtain a badge and a certificate.

Of the special events presented by the Association the most important is 'Champions All', an international tournament held in April at the Empire Pool, Wembley, sponsored by the *Daily Mirror* and to which other countries are invited to send individual competitors. It was at 'Champions All' in 1975 that Nadia Comaneci made her debut in Western Europe.

A new international competition in Britain which promises to be highly popular is the two-day Coca Cola International Gymnastics Tournament for teams and individuals. The first one was held in December 1977.

Perhaps the most prestigious national event is the Champions Cup, also sponsored by the *Daily Mirror*. This takes place in January at the Royal Albert Hall, London, where the six best men and six best girl gymnasts in the country compete. As with 'Champions All', the event takes place in front of a capacity crowd and a huge television audience.

Two recently-established national championships which have sponsors allow girls to compete on just one piece of apparatus rather than on all four. The Lilia-White National Championships, which is a favourite with competitors and audiences alike, is open to girls under 16. The Outline Ladies Gymnastics Championships is for girls of 16 and over. The *Daily Mirror* sends two gymnasts––a boy and a girl aged under 16—to train in the Soviet Union every year. There is keen competition to obtain a place under this scholarship, particularly as the winners' coaches travel with them to learn about Soviet training methods. The

girl winner of the first *Daily Mirror* Scholarship in 1975, Susan Cheesebrough, subsequently represented Britain in the Olympic Games the following year.

Followers of British gymnastics hope that before long the country's gymnastic skills will match the organizational ones. The last ten years have seen a steady improvement in Britain's competitive position. Gymnasts such as Eddie Arnold, Avril Lennox, Ian Neale, Jeff Davis, Karen Leighton and Karen Robb have shown recently that Britons can compete successfully in world-class competition.

While more trained coaches may help to improve British gymnastics faster, it must be remembered that, compared with many other countries which produce top international gymnasts, Britain regards gymnastics as a truly amateur sport. This means that for coaches and gymnasts alike, training must take place in spare time after work. It is heartening to see that, even so, British gymnastics is gaining rapidly on that of countries which not long ago would have defeated Britain by huge scores.

Karen Robb was third in the 1978 'Champions All' in London. She is seen here performing a straddle drop to catch on the bars in the Coca Cola International in 1977.

# Australia and New Zealand

## Don Martin

Karen Ho, the 1978 National Modern Rhythmic Champion of Australia.

Geographical isolation is the greatest drawback to the development of gymnastics in Australia and New Zealand, for it means insufficient international competition for their gymnasts. The other major problem is that, because of the vastness of the Australian continent, the national teams can only meet twice a year.

Both problems are aggravated by shortage of funds, but the lack of finance has to some degree been overcome recently with the introduction of grants from the Federal Government. This aid enables gymnasts and officials to travel more often within Australia and to other countries and also to invite visitors from the leading gymnastic countries of the world.

Australian gymnastics has also benefited as a result of top gymnasts taking up teaching and university positions, from which have followed exchange visits with universities and clubs in other countries.

Australia is divided into seven areas (six States and the Australian Capital Territory). Each has its own president, secretary and technical staff of judges, coaches and organizers directed by the National President, Jim Barry.

In the last three years the national competitions have been rearranged and both men and women now take part in a 10-Level Award Scheme graded according to ability. The men have national competitions at level 7 to 10 and when they reach level 10 they are on to the international requirements of Olympic compulsory exercises. Australian women take part in national competitions at levels 8 to 10, which are classified as follows: level 10—Elite Gold (Olympic requirements); level 9—Silver (modified Olympic requirements); level 8—Bronze (Junior Elite under 14).

These changes have had a tremendous impact on Australian gymnastics by producing physically and mentally prepared gymnasts competing at their ability level rather than in age groupings.

Australia had three individual entries at the Montreal Olympics. Peter Lloyd was placed 81st with a score of 104.75 and Philip Cheetham was 84th with 102.80. They were placed above Jeff Davis of Great Britain, Roberto Richards of Cuba and Fernando Bertrand of Spain. In the Women's Individual Event Wanita Lynch was placed 83rd with 71.20 points, beating two girls from Mexico and one from Spain.

The problems created by the national teams meeting only twice a year are to some extent relieved by close liaison between the national and state coaches. Peter Chen, National Coach of New Zealand, and Boris Bajin, National Coach of Canada, have played leading roles in the advancement of training techniques and coaching methods within Australia.

With the developments brought about by the 10-Level Incentive Award Scheme, a physical preparation programme has been developed to train gymnasts towards the more advanced movements being executed throughout the world.

Australia has at least one major national coaching clinic a year for men's and women's gymnastics and Modern Rhythmics, and state coaches are encouraged to run courses within their areas.

Australia and New Zealand work very closely together for the training of judges in both artistic and rhythmic gymnastics. Judges are tested both at state and national levels and the top judges travel internationally to gain experience for the improvement of judging and its training.

Modern Rhythmic Gymnastics has been going in New Zealand since 1963, the year when this branch of gymnastics was recognized by the F.I.G. The sport was helped along by European coaches coming to New Zealand and by the Danish team travelling in the two islands giving demonstrations.

New Zealand's national coach, Emmy Bellwood of Auckland, trains young women for the New Zealand and World Championships. Modern Rhythmics teams were sent to the Vienna and Berlin Gymnaestradas and the New Zealanders have made appearances in Canada and the United States. A team from New Zealand went to the Cuba World Championships and another team of five flew to Amsterdam for the 1973 World Championships. This team, led by Emmy Bell-

Karen Edelsten, Australian silver level champion of 1978.

wood, consisted of Dale Mercier, Marguerite Johnson, Jeannette Ralfe and Janice Heale. Although Modern Rhythmic Gymnastics is not yet recognized as a competitive sport for the Olympics, New Zealand was asked to send a team for the opening ceremony at Montreal.

Peter Lloyd, one of the three Australian individual entries at the 1976 Montreal Olympics, doing a dislocation on the rings.

# China

## Hua
## Chien-min

Wu-Se-De, shown here in a double pike back somersault, demonstrates that the Chinese are a nation to be reckoned with at the highest possible level in gymnastics, although they do not at present participate in the Olympics or the World Championships.

Gymnastics has seen rapid development since the founding of the People's Republic in 1949. Chinese gymnasts participated in international competitions for the first time at the World Championships in 1958. At the World Championships four years later, they drew the attention of the world's gymnasts by finishing fourth in the men's team total and sixth in the women's team total. At the Asian Games in 1974, China won eight gold medals in gymnastic events, including the men's and women's team events and the women's individual all around event.

At the 1977 World University Games held in August in Sophia, 20-year-old Chinese gymnast Li Yueh-chiu came second in the men's individual free exercise event. He began his performance by turning two backward jack-knife somersaults with a full twist, and landed on the floor, as firm as a nail. No other gymnast present did this routine. With precision, balance and agility, he finished a series of difficult feats, including high somersaults, and drew roars of applause from the spectators.

China was placed third in the men's team total in this competition. Li Yueh-chiu captured the bronze medal in the vault, and Tsai Huan-tsung the bronze medal in the parallel bars. China's national flag was raised on four occasions at the arena.

Tsai Huan-tsung, one of the top gymnasts in China, has won the national championship in the all around event for five successive years, from 1973 to 1977. He won first place in four other events at the 1977 national gymnastics contest. Tsai Huan-tsung, who took a liking to gymnastics as a child, began training in his spare time when he was 12 years old. Training hard and always trying to improve his skills, he became an all arounder in the sport. Two other outstanding men gymnasts are Peng Ya-ping, a young gymnast who excels in all six events, and Hsiung Sung-liang, who is known for his unique movements on the horizontal bar. Both of them participated in the 1977 World University Games.

A group of promising women gymnasts have also come to the fore in China. At the 1977 national contest Chu Cheng, Ma Wen-chu, Wang Ping and Ho Hsiu-min, all aged about 15, executed a series of difficult movements rarely performed by Chinese gymnasts before. Chu Cheng captured the all around championship by defeating Liu Ya-chun, an outstanding young gymnast who won the title in the previous national contest. Chu Cheng, who made her debut at the age of 11 at a national junior gymnastics contest, took part in the National Games in 1975.

Tsai Huan-tsung won the men's all around individual and pommelled horse events in China's 1977 national gymnastics tournament. Excellence is indicated here by his working in between the pommels.

Gymnastics is becoming ever more popular in China. In some places, people exercise on vaulting horses and other equipment they have made from locally available materials. Promising gymnasts are generally selected from among school students, and some primary school children are given special extra-curricular training at the sports schools for juniors established in the larger cities. Those who do well in these spare time sports schools are selected to represent their own provinces, municipalities or regions at national contests. The most distinguished ones are selected to take part in international contests after undergoing a short period of training.

Since the founding of the People's Republic, Chinese gymnasts have toured forty-eight countries in Asia, Africa, Latin America, Europe and America, and have participated on many occasions in world contests. This has enhanced friendship and unity between the people of China and other countries and, while learning a good deal from their counterparts in other countries, Chinese gymnasts have devised some new and difficult movements of their own to share with other nations.

*Opposite:* Liang-Lan Chen at a Chinese display in London in 1977. This body lean is one of the most widely used movements on the floor.

*Above:* It is said that there are 14-year-olds in China who can perform the full Olympic routine on the pommelled horse. Here young boys are being put through their paces.

*Below:* A young Cantonese girl in the first flight of a vault.

China picks out her best gymnasts from those who participate in national gymnastics contests held almost every year since 1953. Many veteran gymnasts are working as coaches or teachers to help bring up a new generation of gymnasts in different parts of the country.

# Canada

## Tom Kinsman

The tradition of vibrant, energetic gymnastics is conveyed by Canada's Karen Kelsall, seen here performing in the Montreal Olympics in 1976.

In July 1976 the Olympic Games were held in Montreal. To the rest of the world, the event was a breathtaking and colourful display of finely-tuned human bodies, and of communications technologies being stressed to their limits. However, to Canadian sport enthusiasts it meant much more: the Montreal Olympics represented a drastic change in Canada's sport perspectives. The opportunity of hosting the world's most significant sporting event was one that could not be missed. The Canadian Government, the Canadian Olympic Association and private businesses came forward with financial and moral support, which made it possible for the governing bodies of the various sports to plan and implement comprehensive national and international programmes for the first time.

Of course the preparation time was too short to expect spectacular Canadian performances at the '76 Games, but what was significant was the increase in Government support for sport and the Canadian public's involvement with international amateur sport. In fact immediately after the Games a new Ministry of Sport and Fitness was created within the Canadian Government. The results of all this activity and support are now beginning to show as Canada's results in world competition are steadily improving. One sport that is showing a phenomenally strong national growth, and hence making an impact on the traditionally European-dominated international scene, is gymnastics.

A new interest in gymnastics has swept the country. Clubs do not seem to be able to open their doors quickly enough to handle all the boys and girls wanting to perform saltos, swings and cartwheels within the exhilarating realms of gymnastics. The media, mesmerized by the feats of Korbut and Comaneci, have acquired a new respect and admiration for the gymnastics performer, and this enthusiasm for the sport has been contagious.

In Canada, private clubs are the foundation of the competitive programme and they produce

*Opposite:* Canadian Sherry Hawko doing an aerial cartwheel on the beam.

most of the National Team athletes. It is in the club system that we find our best trained coaches, providing intensive training programmes in which prospective champions are working up to twenty-five hours per week towards the goal of becoming elite gymnasts.

The Canadian Gymnastics Federation has devised a National Talent Identification Programme for spotting elite gymnasts. The Federation employs a Men's National Coach and a Women's National Coach, who make several trips across Canada per year, looking at the up-and-coming talent. They have developed standard tests and norms of physical ability and performance skill which allow youngsters and their coaches an opportunity to measure their efforts against the standards necessary for high-level involvement with the sport. The tests also allow the National Coaches to identify the most promising gymnasts early enough in their careers for extra attention to be given in a period when good habits and techniques must be learned correctly. The best of these individuals (both gymnast and coach) are brought together annually in a national training camp and given the benefits of working with the National Coach and some of the best coaches in the country. The athlete's gymnastic growth and performance is then monitored as he or she reaches the National Team Programme.

Philip Delesalle, one of the most dedicated of the Canadian gymnasts. He was a medal winner in the 1977 Moscow Riga competitions.

The National Team Programme is planned by the Technical Committees and the National Coaches, together with the coaches of the highest-ranking athletes. Increased funding has allowed athletes and coaches the privilege of travelling to competitions all over the world, an important and costly venture for a country so geographically separated from Europe, where so much of world gymnastics takes place.

National training camps are held regularly, to allow assessment of the top athletes and exchange of information among the coaches. These camps are another high-cost element in the Programme, since the athletes are spread across a country that is approximately 4000 miles wide.

The training of elite gymnasts, however, plays only a small part in the entire gymnastics field in Canada. The Canadian Gymnastics Federation is developing programmes to assist schools, community agencies and clubs in offering gymnastics on a recreational or educational level, with an emphasis on personal enjoyment and health. A simple system of awards for achievement is available and within the reach of the average young person.

One of the tasks facing the Canadian Federation is the recruitment of competent coaches and instructors in a country where gymnastics does not have a rich heritage of expertise to draw on. There is no shortage of talented and interested young people to take part in the sport, but there is

definitely a shortage of qualified coaches.

The National Federation, to remedy this situation, is working out a Coaching Certification Programme which offers training to coaches and instructors at all levels of gymnastics, from recreation to high-performance. Beginning levels of the programme are now running in all ten provinces in Canada, with over 2000 coaches taking the courses. Projects like this will not show immediate results in the international competitive field, but will have long-term benefits, both for Canada's future in world standings and for the growth of gymnastics as a healthful physical pursuit for Canadians.

The 15,000 (only last year it was 8000) members of the Canadian Gymnastics Federation represent only a small percentage of the participants in the sport, primarily those in private clubs. Participants in schools, recreational and community organizations are many times more numerous. These enthusiasts are treated every year to a number of top-class events in Canada. Annually, each summer, the ten provinces compete in National Championships on both a Senior and a Junior level. This allows the Canadian public to see some of the best Canadian gymnasts, either live or on television. Fifteen-year-old Karen Kelsall, who was the youngest competitor in the '76 Olympics, is the current National Women's Senior Champion and continues to bring honours to Canada. In 1977 she defeated opponents from the U.S.S.R., Rumania and other top-ranking gymnastic countries in the well-known Coca Cola Invitational (formerly Milk-Meet), an international meet held every year in Toronto and Calgary. This competition, drawing a crowd of over 18,000 spectators to Toronto's Maple Leaf Gardens every year, reflects the rise of Canadian interest in gymnastics.

The Senior National Men's Champion, Philip Delesalle, is the most successful gymnast Canada has ever produced. He has competed all over the world and on various occasions has defeated Olympic and World Champions. In 1977 he was asked by the F.I.G. to participate in a tour of Brazil—an invitation limited to the world's best gymnasts.

Philip and Karen represent a new breed of gymnasts coming out of Canada—young, dynamic gymnasts with carefully-programmed training schedules. They are cresting a wave of younger, well-disciplined athletes, who will in their turn reflect Canada's advancement in the sport. They and the other Canadian Olympic gymnasts showed the beginnings of Canada's improvement when all of them, the whole Canadian team, achieved higher than a 9.0 average in Olympic competition: a fine performance for a country that is a relative newcomer to the exciting, challenging and beautiful world of gymnastics.

# South Africa

## Louis Wessels

Kathy Myburgh, one of South Africa's top gymnasts, practising on the beam. Despite South Africa's isolation in world sport, her gymnasts take part regularly in competition in Europe, Asia and the United States.

It was decided to bring overseas gymnasts to South Africa to improve the local standard of gymnastics after South Africa's participation in the Olympic Games in Helsinki in 1952 and the World Championships in Rome in 1954, when it became apparent to the South African Gymnastics Union that South Africa was lagging behind other nations thanks to her lack of international experience.

The first visit of a top gymnast to South Africa was by the German champion Helmuth Bantz in 1956. In 1955 he had gained third place in the European Championships and in 1956 had been awarded the Olympic gold medal for vaulting in Melbourne. A year later the Swede William Thoresson was invited to South Africa, and in 1958 the Spaniard Joachim Blume. The visit of the two Japanese Takashi Ono and Takashi Mitsukuri in 1962 was a milestone for gymnastics in South Africa and an unforgettable experience for all who had the good fortune of seeing them in action. Danielle Coulon, seven times winner of the French women's title, was the first well-known overseas woman gymnast to visit South Africa. Her visit helped considerably to arouse interest in the sport, particularly among women.

South African gymnasts have taken part in overseas competitions, including the Olympic Games and the World Championships, as frequently as possible. The last time the Springboks (the South African national team) were in action was at the Olympic Games in 1960 and the World Championships in 1966.

Much is being done to improve the quality of South African gymnastics. The first top-ranking coaches—Dr J. Cronstedt and Miss Ulla Berg, both of them Swedes—were brought to South Africa in 1966 by the Gymnastics Union. A national course for coaches was held in Bloemfontein and on that occasion a special committee was appointed to give constant attention to the training of gymnasts and their preparation for top competitions. Other overseas coaches who visited South Africa were George Chautemps (France), Jack Guntard (Switzerland) and Don Peters, Paul Ziert, Bill Coco, Jim Gault and Abie Grossfeld of the United States. Since 1964 courses for coaches, as well as for judges, have been held regularly in all parts of the country.

Until recently, the non-white inhabitants of South Africa showed little or no interest in gymnastics. This, however, has changed and in recent years, with the assistance of local sports administrators and overseas coaches, interest in the sport has been growing, particularly among the coloured people of the Cape Province. All racial groups in South Africa belong to the South African Gymnastics Union and compete in club, provincial and national competitions.

Every year all fourteen regional associations affiliated to the Union take part in national open championships, and championships graded according to age and ability. Through these associations control is exercised over the 10,000 registered gymnasts in South Africa.

Altogether 68 men and women have already gained their Springbok colours in gymnastics. The leading women gymnasts at present are Kathy Myburgh, Gigi de Jongh, Debbie Skjöldhammer and Caroline Hossack, while the top men are Alwyn Gerber, Kobus Stander, Chris de Wet and Willie Krause.

# Japan

## Toshikata Tagawa

The effort involved in high-class gymnastics is reflected in the facial expression of Mitsuo Tsukahara as he moves into the twisting double back somersault. At 30 he is one of the old hands of Japanese gymnastics.

To the Japanese gymnastics is an attitude of mind, much as in the traditional Japanese systems of self-defence, Judo, Karate and Kendo. Japanese coaches of course make use of scientific approaches, but they do not rely on them entirely. They place most emphasis on the maintenance of coolness and tranquillity of mind on the part of the gymnast in every situation.

Japanese gymnasts are taught that there is no one to help them during the warm-up and competition period. On the podium they will be alone and must depend on themselves.

Coaches stress to the gymnasts that the competition must not be regarded as a new and different experience. They are drilled to make practice like competition and competition like practice. It is in fact very difficult for a gymnast to keep a cool head during a competition, but Japan's outstanding men gymnasts do achieve this tranquillity and strength of mind. They are not afraid of making mistakes during their performances and that is the secret of their strength at the Olympic Games and World Championships.

A Japanese men's team took part in the Olympics for the first time in Los Angeles in 1932, two years after the formation of the Gymnastics Federation of Japan in Tokyo in 1930. Japan was placed bottom—fifth out of the five teams that took part.

A Japanese men's team went to the Berlin Olympics in 1936, and another to Helsinki in 1952. On the latter occasion there was a team of only five gymnasts, but they were placed fifth out of 23 teams from all over the world.

At the 1954 World Championships in Rome, the 1956 Melbourne Olympics and the 1958 World Championships in Moscow, the Japanese men's team came second. Finally in Rome in 1962 they took first place. Since then the Japanese men's team have won every Olympic Games to give them five in a row, and they have also won four World Championships.

So Japan's male gymnasts have stayed at the top for seventeen years and it is likely that their team will continue to win the Olympic Games and World Championships in the future.

A Japanese women's team participated in the Olympic Games for the first time in 1956 at Melbourne and they came sixth. At the World Championships in Prague in 1962, they came third and they stayed in this position at the 1964 Olympics in Tokyo and at the World Championships in Dortmund in 1966. But, after that, the team's results declined and at the Olympic Games in Montreal in 1976 they were placed eighth. The Japanese women's technical committee must reexamine their approach to training and take steps to strengthen the women's team.

The president of the Japan Federation is Yoshinori Maeda and the general secretary is

Satoko Okazaki of Japan on the beam. Japanese women gymnasts are striving to reach the same exalted position in world gymnastics as their men.

Hiroshi Nosaka. The federation has two main committees, executive and technical. There is a technical committee for both men and women, a research committee and a committee for Rhythmic Gymnastics. The committees meet about twice a month and are usually composed of about ten members mostly consisting of professors or lecturers at universities or colleges or of schools' physical education teachers.

Schools gymnastics forms the basis of training in Japan, although recently there has been a growth in the number of private clubs.

Outstanding competitors develop at college or university, but they will have acquired fundamental abilities at school.

Physical education instructors at school and college all have a general knowledge of the gymnastic training method. The 'direct' and 'indirect' methods are two of many varieties.

In the direct method, the gymnast is first taught each phase of a movement and then he is encouraged to put together the several elements. For instance, the handspring on the floor can be divided into three phases, the hopping phase, the pre-flight and push-off phase, and the post-flight and landing phase.

Hisato Igarashi is one of the young gymnasts selected to protect the Japanese Olympic title from capture by the Russians in 1980. Here he is performing a rear vault over the horizontal bar.

Eizo Kenmotsu, probably the toughest gymnast ever produced by Japan, is seen here performing the Diamidov turn on the parallel bars, watched by Yukio Endo.

In the indirect method the various moves are graded from easy to difficult and the gymnast is taught three or four elements which are then put together into stages of a routine.

Many national championship meetings are held from early summer to autumn and the largest is the All Japan Championships usually staged between mid-October and early November. Only competitors who were marked at over 85% points in the previous National Championships can take part. All Japan becomes the first elimination match when there are Olympic Games or World Championships the following year.

The Nippon Broadcasting Corporation Cup Competitions are usually held in mid-June with 36 men and 24 women competitors selected according to the individual scores in the previous All Japan Championships.

There are other championships as follows: the Middle School Championships for 12- to 15-year-old boys and girls; the High School Championships for 15- to 18-year-old boys and girls; and the Collegiate Championships for men and women between the ages of 18 and 23.

The *Chunichi* Cup International is an invitation tournament sponsored by the Japanese newspaper *Chunichi*. It is generally held at the beginning of November at Nagoya, in the Aichi prefecture. The Japanese federation and *Chunichi* invite elite men and women competitors from all over the world—East and West Germany, Hungary, Rumania, Czechoslovakia, France, the United States, the Soviet Union etc. The competition is designed to promote friendship and technical exchange between Japan and foreign countries. *Chunichi* is televised and the TV company guarantees funds to the federation. The main income of the federation depends upon this competition.

# Rumania

## Nicolae Vieru

Nadia Comaneci in an aerial cartwheel on the beam.

*Above:* The impact Nadia Comaneci made in Skien in 1972 when she won the European Championships remains to this day. This photograph gives some indication of the strength and positive range of movement in the hip girdle.

*Opposite:* Svetlana Grozdova doing a Valdez passing through the handstand position. Her extraordinary range of movement can be seen in the shoulder extension at this point in the movement.

Sport enjoyed a tremendous resurgence in Rumania following the end of World War II: facilities were made available in schools, universities, workshops, factories and villages. Gymnastics, too, entered a new phase of development, being popular especially among children and young people. Since 1947 National Gymnastics Championships for seniors have been organized on a regular basis with a team title, an individual combined title, and a title for the uneven parallel (asymmetric) bars and beam. Similarly there are annual National Championships for children, schools, juniors and universities as well as the 'Rumanian Cup'—the International Championship which enjoys worldwide prestige. This championship was first held in 1958 and its twentieth meeting takes place this year. Over the years, top ranking stars from all over the world have participated in this competition.

The first Rumanian gymnastics club was founded in 1868 in the capital, Bucharest. The Rumanian Gymnastics Federation, comprising eighteen clubs, was established in 1905 and became affiliated to the F.I.G. in 1907. Today the Federation consists of 376 clubs of all kinds—top-level clubs, school clubs, student clubs, workers' clubs and village clubs. Together they have a total membership of 18,000, of which 4000 take part in competitions. The Federation is the sole body

*Below:* Teodora Ungureanu doing a free walk over during the floor exercise competition at the 1976 'Champions All' in London which she won for the second year in succession.

*Pages 118-19:* Nadia Comaneci doing a straddle forward somersault from the top bar back onto the top bar.

*Opposite:* Maria Filatova at the demonstration in London of the Soviet team in 1977 with the puckish movements that have come to be seen as a mark of her performances.

responsible for regulating and supervising gymnastics in Rumania. It has its own income, which comes from members' and associate members' subscriptions, from competition receipts, television fees and state grants.

Rumanian gymnasts have enjoyed considerable successes in international competitions but the most notable are, without doubt, those gained at the 1976 Montreal Olympics. Nadia Comaneci won three gold medals (for the individual combined, the uneven parallel (asymmetric) bars and the beam, making her overall Olympic Champion), a team silver medal, and a bronze for her floor exercise. Teodora Ungureanu won two silver medals (team and uneven (asymmetric) parallel bars) and a bronze medal for the beam, while the male gymnast Dan Grecu won a bronze medal for the rings. The women's team won a silver medal. Other recent victories include Nadia Comaneci's four gold medals and one silver in the European Championships in Skien, Norway, in 1975, and the retention of her title in Prague in 1977. Dan Grecu became World Champion on the rings in 1975 and World Student Champion on the rings in 1973 and 1977.

Rumania's success in women's gymnastics goes back further than the recent past. The Rumanian team won the bronze medal at the Olympic Games in Melbourne in 1956 and Rome in 1960 and at the World Championships in 1958. Two stars of that era, Elena Leustean and Sonia Ivan, climbed the victor's rostrum on numerous occasions at the Olympics and the European Championships during the decade 1956-66.

The Rumanian school of gymnastics is world famous, its success owing much to progressive theories on the selection and early training of children. These brought about the foundation of the gymnastically-orientated high school in the town of Gheorghiu Dej where Nadia Comaneci and Teodora Ungureanu trained.

Inspired by the generation of Nadia and Teodora, women's gymnastics has blossomed in many other towns, from which will soon appear new names in Rumanian gymnastics.

The tradition and experience of the Rumanian school, and the capability and enthusiasm of expert coaches, is a sure guarantee that in the future Rumanian gymnastics will reinforce its reputation and renown in world-class competition.

Mihail Bors executing a Voronin Hop on the horizontal bar. Although one hears comparatively little about Rumanian male gymnasts, the records show an outstanding number of achievements in recent years.

# Gymnastics for Health and Fitness

When watching a gymnastics competition, we often tend to forget how many daily hours of training, from early childhood onwards, have been responsible for producing the agile body and supreme mental control that makes a first-class gymnast. Athough most of us can never hope to perform a successful handstand, let alone a flic-flac, we can participate in the greater enjoyment of life that regular exercise brings. With a fit, healthy body we will look better, work better, play better. We will also have more of a chance of resisting heart disease and some of the other ailments of 20th-century life.

Training in a gymnasium is becoming a more and more popular way of keeping fit among both men and women today, but even if you do not have time or the inclination to go to a gym, there are many exercises that can be done in the home just as effectively.

There are numerous keep-fit programmes available, and we do not aim to set out a new one here. Which one you choose depends on your own preferences (and in case of any doubt at all you must consult your doctor). The sample exercises shown here are intended merely as 'tasters', to convince at least a few readers that the reality of exercise is not as grim as the prospect. All these exercises can be done by men and women.

Yoga is an alternative form of exercise that many people find particularly suited to the tension and demands of contemporary life. It is best described as a means of total physical and mental control.

Yoga is a slow, graceful means of exercise. It places no value on strain or effort, but rather conserves energy, easing, persuading, applying gentle pressure and thus leading, its practitioners claim, to a supple and healthy body, to inner tranquility and, for really dedicated devotees, to spiritual attainment.

## Warming-up Exercises

These should be done at the start of an exercise session. Do each one a few times at first and gradually increase the number of repetitions.

## Side Bends

Stand up with your feet as wide apart as is comfortable and put your hands on your hips. Bend your body, first to the right, then to the left. Do not move your head; keep it at right angles to your shoulders. You should develop a continuous movement—bend right, straighten up, bend left and so on.

## Kneeling Backbend

Kneel on the floor, raising your heels and keeping your hands on your hips. Now bend back as far as you can, pushing your head back at the same time. Then return to your starting position.

## Ankle Reach

Stand with your feet as far apart as is comfortable and rest both your palms against the front part of your upper right thigh. Bend forwards, letting the weight of your trunk move down towards your right thigh. Slide your hands down towards your right ankle. Repeat the exercise on the left side of your body.

## Knee Bend

Stand with your body erect, your arms extended in front of you and your feet together. Lift yourself up on the balls of your feet. Bend down so that you are squatting, keeping your heels raised. Then straighten your legs and return to the starting position.

# Strength Exercises

This group of exercises is intended to strengthen specific parts of your body. Do each one a few times at first and gradually increase the number of repetitions.

## Table Press-up

Stand in front of a table with your feet apart. Place both hands on the table edge, palms down; your arms should be straight so that your hands are shoulder width apart. Now bend your arms and lean forwards so that your chest touches the table. Straightening your arms, return to the starting position.

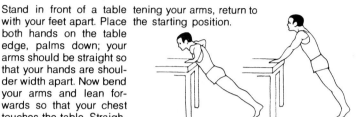

## Squat Jump

With your hands by your sides, put one foot in front of the other so that the heel of one touches the toe of the other. Now leap as high as you can in the air, swapping the position of your feet. Land in a squatting position, with your heels raised and the tips of your fingers touching the floor. Straighten up and repeat the exercise.

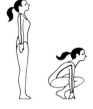

## Backward Leg Stretch

Stand straight with your hands by your sides. Squat, raising your heels and placing your hands palms down on the floor, and then extend your legs back as far as possible, keeping them straight. Return first to the squat, then to the starting position.

## Running on the Spot

Stand with your arms hanging loosely by your sides. Simply run on the same spot. Do not lift your knees and feet very high at first. Try to do this exercise for half a minute at first. Gradually increase to several minutes, at the same time lifting your knees higher.

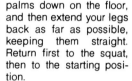

## The Cobra

Lie on your front so that your feet rest on the floor touching each other. Bend your elbows so that your finger tips are level with your shoulders. Bring your forehead down to the floor and push your chin forwards so that your neck forms a straight line with the upper part of your body.

Now breathe in and lift your head and shoulders from the floor. Count up to 10, put your chin on the floor again and breathe out.

# Yoga Exercises

Shown here are a few of the best-known yoga positions.

## The Tree

Start by standing straight with your arms by your sides. Bend your right leg and put the sole of your right foot as high as you can on the inside of your left thigh. Stretch your arms out as far as possible. Look straight ahead and hold the pose for as long as you can. Repeat the movement, putting your left foot against your right thigh.

## Relaxation Pose

This position above all others sums up the philosophy and aims of yoga. It should bring perfect relaxation to mind and body. Lie on your back. Your feet should be a little apart, your arms by your sides, palms up. Do not hold yourself stiffly, but let your head and neck relax, without rolling to one side. Place your tongue behind your lower teeth. Start and finish each yoga session by lying like this for a few minutes.

# Picture Acknowledgements

Permission to reproduce photographs was kindly given by the following. Page numbers of colour illustrations are given in bold type.

All-Sport Photographic Limited: 10, 19, 20-21, 25, 29, 60, 92, 94 (right), **107**, **108** (photos Tony Duffy); **12**, 24 (photos Don Morley); 59, 61, 115 (photos Mark Moylan); **98** (photo Steve Powell). Courtesy of *The Australian Gymnast:* 102, 103 (above). Alan Burrows: 4 (both), **9**, 13, 14, 23, 30, 82, 84 (above), 89, 99, 100 (both), 101, 103 (below), 109, 116 (below), **117**, **120**. Courtesy of the Canadian Gymnastics Federation: 110. Courtesy of China Features: 105, 106 (above). Albrecht Gaebele: 2-3, 27, 84 (below), **85**, **86**, **95**, **96-97**, 104, 106 (below), 114 (both), 116 (above), **118-19**, 121. Yoichi Hirade: 1, 112, 113. Courtesy of *International Gymnast:* 5, **11**, 88, 90, 91. The Mansell Collection: 8. Novosti Press Agency: 17, 93 (below). Radio Times Hulton Picture Library: 7 (both), 16. Norbert Smyk: 83, 87, 93 (above), 94 (left). Courtesy of *Top Sport:* 111.

Line drawings by Laurence Jackson Associates.

Tables on pages 20 and 22 by kind permission of *International Gymnast.*

# Bibliography

Carter, E. Russell *Gymnastics for Girls and Women* Englewood Cliffs, N.J., Prentice-Hall, 1968; London, 1969.

Edwards, Vannie *Tumbling* Philadelphia, W. B. Saunders, 1969; Eastbourne, 1969.

Frederick, A. B. *Gymnastics for Women* Iowa, William C. Brown Co., 1969.

Prestidge, Pauline *Better Gymnastics* London, Kaye and Ward, 1977.

Ryan, F. *Gymnastics for Girls* New York, Viking Press, 1976; London, Penguin, 1976.

Stuart, N. *Gymnastics for Men* London, Stanley Paul & Co. Ltd. (Hutchinson Publishing Group, Ltd.), 1978.

Taylor, B. and Zivic, T. *Olympic Gymnastics for Men and Women* Englewood Cliffs, N.J., Prentice-Hall, 1972.

Warren, Meg *The Book of Gymnastics* London, Arthur Barker, 1972; New York, 1972.

Wettstone, E. (ed.) *Gymnastics Safety Manual* issued by the United States Gymnastics Safety Association, Washington. Published by Pennsylvania State University Press, 1977.

# Notes on Contributors

PETER AYKROYD is an educational journalist. Over the last seven years he has been a press officer for gymnastics at club, regional, national and international level. He is Event Press Officer for the British Amateur Gymnastics Association and is editor of the Association's official journal *The Gymnast*.

URSEL BAER is an international gymnastics judge. She has officiated at the Rome, Munich and Montreal Olympics, several World Championships and international matches in Britain and abroad.

FRANK BARE is Executive Director of the United States Gymnastics Federation and Vice President of the International Gymnastics Federation.

JENNY BOTT is Chairperson of the British Amateur Gymnastics Association's Modern Rhythmic Gymnastics Committee and British National Coach for Modern Rhythmics.

HUA CHIEN-MIN is a sports journalist working for 'China Features' in Peking.

ARTHUR GANDER is Honorary President of the International Federation of Gymnastics.

GIORGIO GARUFI has held the post of Professor of Artistic Gymnastics at the University of Physical Education in Naples since 1960. For some years he was Chairman of Adjudicators, and Regional Technical Director of Artistic Gymnastics to the Italian Federation of Gymnastics and has written three books on Artistic Gymnastics.

DR JOSEF GÖHLER is the International Editor of *International Gymnast*.

MURIEL GROSSFELD is a well known United States gymnast who, among other successes, held the United States National Floor Exercise Championship for eight consecutive years. She now has her own gymnastics school.

TOM KINSMAN is the Coaching Development Coordinator for the Canadian Gymnastics Federation.

DON MARTIN is Coaching Coordinator for Queensland, Australia.

TONY MURDOCK is Development Officer to the British Amateur Gymnastics Association.

JACK SCRIVENER is an international gymnastics judge officiating at several World Championships and at the Munich Olympics. He judges most senior international and national matches in Great Britain and many abroad.

NIK STUART is the British Men's National Coach for the British Amateur Gymnastics Association. For nine consecutive years (1954-63) he was gymnastics champion of Great Britain.

TOSHIKATA TAGAWA has been Vice President of the research committee of the Japanese Gymnastics Association, and Chief Editor of the journal of the committee since 1976.

PETER TATLOW is a freelance sports writer for several British national newspapers, covering gymnastics, English county cricket and women's lacrosse. He is a profile writer and match reporter for *The Gymnast*, the British gymnastics journal, and a regular contributor to *International Gymnast*.

CLIFF TEMPLE is a journalist and broadcaster. He is gymnastics and track-and-field correspondent for the London *Sunday Times* and track-and-field correspondent for *The Times*.

YURI TITOV is President of the International Federation of Gymnastics and head of the Soviet Union's Sports Committee's Gymnastics Section. He was Olympic Champion several times and twice gymnastics champion of the Soviet Union.

NICOLAE VIERU is General Secretary of the Rumanian Federation of Gymnastics.

LOUIS WESSELS is Editor of *Topsport*, South Africa's leading sports magazine. He is also author of three novels for children, all with sporting themes.

# Glossary

**A.B.C. parts:** Difficulty ratings of individual movements. A is the lowest, C the highest.

**Amplitude:** Maximum possible size of movement, e.g. height, swing, stretch, reach etc.

**Artistic gymnastics:** Olympic gymnastics on four pieces of apparatus for women and on six pieces of apparatus for men.

**Asymmetric bars** (*See* Uneven parallel bars)

**Back support:** Body resting on the upper thighs in front of the bar.

**Balance beam:** Wooden beam on metal supports. Height: 1.20 metres (about 4 feet 9 inches); length: 5 metres (about 16 feet 5 inches); width: 10 centimetres (about 4 inches).

**Cartwheel:** Rotation of the body sideways through the inverted position on the hands, onto the feet.

**Code of points:** Book containing the rules for judging gymnasts. It gives specific deductions for specific faults.

**Compulsory exercise:** Exercise composed by the F.I.G. which must be performed exactly as prescribed.

**Connections:** Movements linking together individual elements of an exercise.

**Crossgrasp:** One hand in undergrasp, one hand in overgrasp.

**Dismount:** Last movement of an exercise when the gymnast descends from the apparatus.

**Element:** Single movement in an exercise.

**F.I.G.:** International Federation of Gymnastics.

**Floor:** Area of the floor measuring 12 metres × 12 metres (about 13 square yards), marked off and covered with carpeted wooden boards or mats.

**Front support:** Hips supported on the bar.

**Front vault:** Vault over the horse with straight body facing it.

**Handspring:** Forward jump onto the hands with immediate repulsion forwards onto the feet.

**Handstand:** Body supported on hands at 180 degrees.

**Hip circle:** Circular movement round the bar with the hips against the bar.

**Hold position:** Pose that is held for three seconds.

**Horizontal bar:** Metal bar supported by five metal poles. Height: 2.55 metres (about 8 feet 4 inches); width: 2.40 metres (about 8 feet).

**Horse:** Flat-surfaced, leather-covered rectangular body on wooden supports. Height: 1.20 metres (about 4 feet 9 inches); length: 1.60 metres (about 5 feet 3 inches).

**Inverted hang:** Body suspended upside-down from the hands on the still rings.

**Kip:** Movement of the body so that feet come towards the head, followed by an extension movement with which the body is elevated to front support. Usually performed on the bars.

**Linkages:** Connections between the moves of an exercise.

**Modern Rhythmic Gymnastics:** Team and individual exercises done on the floor to music, with or without hand apparatus.

**Mount:** Method of getting onto the apparatus to start an exercise.

**Movement:** One part of an exercise.

**Open scoring:** System of scoring as in ice-skating where marks given by each individual judge are made visible to the audience.

**Overgrasp:** Hands grasping bars, palms down.

**Parallel bars:** Wooden bars parallel to each other and at the same height supported by adjustable metal poles. Length: 3.50 metres (about 11 feet 6 inches); height: 1.50-2.30 metres (about 4 feet 11 inches to about 7 feet 7 inches); distance apart: 43-52 centimetres (about 1 foot 5 inches to about 1 foot 8 inches).

**Pike:** Position with the body folded at the waist and straight legs.

**Pirouette:** Rotation around the long axis of the body.

**Podium:** Large platform on which competition or display is held.

**Pommelled horse:** Leather-covered wooden horse with straight body and handles (pommels) screwed into it. Height: 1.10 metres (about 3 feet 7 inches); length: 1.60 metres (about 5 feet 3 inches).

**Rear lying hang:** Hang with arms grasping the high bar and buttocks on the low bar.

**Rear stand:** Stand with the back to the apparatus.

**Rear vault:** Vault with the rear of the body facing the bar.

**Referee:** A neutral judge in overall charge of the judging of a competition who arbitrates if arguments occur.

**R.O.V.:** Risk, originality and virtuosity increase the value ot an exercise.

**Routine:** Sequence of movements forming an exercise.

**Saddle:** Middle part of the pommelled horse.

**Salto:** A somersault rotating around the horizontal axis with upward flight and without hand support.

**Sokol:** Group run by the church.

**Splits:** A leg movement with the angle between the legs at 180 degrees.

**Sports acrobatics:** Competitions in tumbling and acrobatics, the latter performed individually or in groups.

**Still rings:** Stationary rings supported from ropes and straps. Height above floor: 2.55 metres (about 8 feet 4 inches); total height of apparatus: 5.50 metres (about 18 feet).

**Straddle:** Movement with straight legs held apart with a wide angle between them.

**Tuck:** Body position with legs bent up to the chest.

**Tumble:** Perform somersaults, flic-flacs etc.

**Turners:** People who run gym clubs; derived from the German *Turner*, meaning gymnast.

**Undergrasp:** Grasping the bars from underneath, palms upwards.

**Uneven parallel bars:** Wooden bars on metal supports, parallel to each other but one high and one low. High bar: 2.30 metres (about 7 feet 7 inches) from the ground; low bar: 1.50 metres (about 5 feet) from the ground.

**Uprise:** Straight body swinging upon straight arms to front support.

**Upstart** (*See* Kip)

**Vault:** Body flying over the horse.

**Voluntary exercise:** Exercise constructed of movements selected by the gymnast or coach.

**Walkover:** A movement rotating forward or backward round the shoulder axis, with momentary hand support in the inverted position.

# Index